Anti-Inflammatory Diet Cookbook

Dairy Free, Gluten Free, Sugar Free Recipes to Heal The Immune System, Achieve Permanent Weight Loss And Heal & Detox Your Body

Table of Contents

Conclusion

Introduction

Inflammation occurs as a way for your body to defend itself from infection and irritants. It is for this reason why the area around your wound swells up because there are white blood cells and immune system cells that prevent the infection from spreading elsewhere. While inflammation is a sign that the body is fighting a disease, a situation of constant and prolonged inflammation can seriously affect your health conditions. Chronic inflammation is the reason why people suffer from a lot of diseases such as cancer, diabetes, obesity, and many others. Chronic inflammation is indicative that the body is exposed to infection or injury for a long time. Moreover, it can also mean long-term exposure to irritants, including industrial chemicals or pollution.

Because people are now constantly exposed to irritants, infection, and other things that may cause inflammation, many people suffer from different diseases. If not treated properly, it can lead to a debilitating life. As someone working in the healthcare industry, I have seen so many people who suffer from chronic inflammation. While there are medicines that can help lower down inflammation, eating foods that are anti-inflammatory in nature can help improve quality of life. This is where the Anti-Inflammatory Diet comes in.

Based on my experience in the healthcare industry, I can say that the anti-inflammatory diet is the healthiest diet that people can take advantage of to significantly improve and preserve good health conditions. It encourages people to consume foods that can lower down the inflammation in the body.

I developed this book following the Anti-Inflammatory Diet because I believe that eating the right kind of foods can help reduce chronic inflammation. Wouldn't you think that life is better if you can improve your condition with food? Although there are so many books about the Anti-Inflammatory Diet out there, this book provides you with simple information that you can use to jumpstart this particular diet regimen. Moreover, this book also contains simple and easy-to-follow recipes for everyone. The thing is that I have included everything that you need to know about the Anti-Inflammatory Diet in this book, but I want to make sure that all readers can understand the concepts of this particular diet.

I have designed this book for people who suffer from chronic inflammation and want to improve their condition not only through medicine but also diet. So, if you suffer from rheumatoid arthritis and other diseases caused by inflammation, then you can benefit from this book. But more than those who suffer from inflammation, this diet is also applicable to people who want to live a healthy lifestyle. In a nutshell, this book is for everyone.

But let me remind you that while the Anti-Inflammatory Diet may help improve the condition of people who suffer from chronic inflammation, it does not completely heal individuals but only reduce the flare-ups. Having said this, you should not only rely on this diet alone, but you should also exercise, live a healthy lifestyle, take your medication, and consult with your medical practitioner if you want to improve your condition. But at least this diet will help jumpstart your way to a healthy life.

Chapter 1. Basic Principles Of The Anti Inflammatory Diet

What is the Anti-Inflammatory Diet?

The anti-inflammatory diet is a practical, healthy way of eating that treats and prevents inflammation associated with many chronic conditions and illnesses. Inflammation occurs in the body to fight disease or infection, though it can happen when there is the presence of autoimmune conditions that can trigger unnecessary flare-ups, causing pain and discomfort. When inflammation becomes a regular occurrence itself as a faulty action (as a result of a health condition, but not to heal the body), it can be a serious hindrance in feeling and functioning well. Preventing inflammation can be done successfully through diet, and this includes significant relief from many conditions, including arthritis, psoriasis, colitis, inflammatory bowel disease, and respiratory conditions (asthma, bronchitis). Due to the nutrient-richness of this diet, there are further benefits including significant weight loss and the successful treatment of diabetes (regulating insulin levels), heart disease, lupus, and heart disease. Metabolism and an overall sense of feeling well are further advantages of the anti-inflammatory diet.

Top Anti-Inflammatory Foods

One of the most effective methods in treating inflammation is diet. Building a diet that is rich in nutrients and ingredients that halt or prevent inflammation is key to a more productive, healthy lifestyle. There are some key foods and nutrients to include in your everyday meal plans:

Tomatoes

A versatile fruit, and often considered a vegetable, tomatoes are an excellent source of vitamins and fiber. They can be added to a wide variety of meals, including pasta, salads, and sandwiches, or simply enjoyed on their own. Easily enjoyed raw, stewed, or pureed into a sauce, adding tomatoes to your diet, if you haven't already, is both a healthy and tasty way to improve your diet.

Extra Virgin Olive Oil (preferably cold pressed)

Containing healthy fats, extra virgin olive oil is an excellent choice for many dishes, including sauces, marinades, and for use in cooking. Using extra virgin olive oil in everyday cooking is a great option, and it's relatively easy and inexpensive to buy extra virgin olive oil, which is available in most grocery stores (I would say inexpensive considering its benefits for your health) . Always choose the dark bottle, which helps the oil preserve its freshness. Extra virgin Olive oil is high in monounsaturated fats, which are the healthiest variety. It protects against heart disease, prevents strokes, and improves cognitive function, in addition to having anti-inflammatory properties.

Olives

Olives are tasty and an excellent source of vitamin E, as well as many other antioxidants. They make a great addition to salads, sandwiches, or as a snack with low-fat cheese or vegetables. Olives contain a lot of healthy fats and are a staple in Mediterranean dishes, which is one of the top reasons why Mediterranean cuisine is considered one of the healthiest in the world. Adding just a small portion of olives to your diet can make a significant impact on your health.

Dark Leafy Green Vegetables

Spinach, arugula, and kale are top-notch foods in the anti-inflammatory food group and have a significant impact on many other body functions. They contain vitamins K and C, iron, magnesium, and calcium. Dark greens also contain a lot of antioxidants, which is key to giving them anti-inflammatory powers. Adding any one or all of these leafy foods to your diet is a sure way to improving your diet and health.

Berries and Citrus Fruits

Rich in antioxidants, fiber, and delicious, fruits are an excellent choice for reducing inflammation associated with disease and chronic conditions. While they are seasonal and their availability can vary, certain fruits can be purchased frozen or fresh. They are high in vitamin C and often cited for preventing colds and improving immunity function. Berries are versatile in that they are easy to eat as a snack on their own, though can be added to a variety of recipes, including smoothies, desserts, puddings, and salads.

Nuts and seeds

Almonds, hazelnuts, cashews, pecans, walnuts, and pistachios are among some of the many delicious and nutrient-heavy nuts that can be easily added or supplemented to your diet. If you are vegan, you'll want to include as many nuts and seeds in your diet as possible to get the most out of the nutrients they contain such as protein, fiber, omega 6 and 3 fats, and many vitamins and minerals, including iron, magnesium, and vitamin E. Just a small dose each day can make a significant difference in your health. Nuts and seeds, including chia seeds, pumpkin, sesame, and sunflower seeds, also contain a high number of vitamins and minerals, making them an ideal topping or ingredient in salads, desserts, baked goods, or as a snack on their own.

Fish

Fatty fish, such as salmon, is an excellent source of protein, calcium, and healthy fats. To reduce inflammation, focus on eating salmon and tuna, as both are high in protein, calcium, and healthy fats and contain no sugars or carbohydrates, which contribute to a lot of health conditions. If you are accustomed to eating red meat frequently, slowly replacing some of your beef or pork dishes with salmon or tuna is a great idea, as it reduces the number of inflammatory foods and gives you a good reason to try new recipes! When shopping for fish, always aim for fresh or frozen fish. If you choose canned salmon or tuna, choose fresh catch and fish in general that are naturally sourced, so that it is a higher quality.

Other fish to consider trying and adding to your diet include mackerel, sardines, and white fish, which are also high in protein, calcium and healthy fats.

Coffee

As much as some studies and opinions target coffee as unhealthy, it has benefits that we may not realize until we read about them. Many people avoid coffee because of the effects of caffeine, though in moderate portions, it can reap many benefits. These are discussed further in the drinks and beverages section of the book, which includes some options for enjoying coffee and other hot drinks.

Foods to Avoid: Inflammatory Foods

Refined Foods

In general, all foods that are processed and high in carbohydrates should be avoided or limited as much as possible. If you find yourself craving a box of cookies or a bag of potato chips, skip the snack aisle completely. Instead, look for dried fruits, nuts, and seeds as a healthier way to fulfill your craving. Processed foods offer little to no nutritional benefits, and often contain a lot of artificial additives and hidden sugars.

Soda and Sugary Beverages

Sweetened iced teas, soda, and juices should be avoided. Sugary beverages can become addictive and difficult to replace with water or tea, which are better options, though there are some alternatives to consider, such as unsweetened iced teas, low carb sweetened sodas and sparkling water with natural fruit flavoring. Avoid diet sodas, which contain harmful artificial sweeteners, and instead, search for drinks that contain stevia (a low carb sweetener) or natural options, such as honey or syrup.

Red Meat

In moderation, small portions of red meat can contribute to a healthy diet. It's important to minimize or reduce the portion and alternate with other protein options such as poultry, fish, and tofu (as well as other vegan substitutes). On the other hand, consuming large portions of beef, pork, etc. can lead to heart disease and high blood pressure, especially if you don't eat enough plant-based foods. Balance is key, and while eliminating red meat completely is ideal, it can also be significantly reduced with good results.

Deep-Fried Foods

French fries, fried meats, and even deep-fried vegetables should avoid as much as possible. The taste and texture may be tempting, though these foods contain trans fats or "unhealthy" fats that contribute to many diseases, such as cancer, heart conditions, and asthma. If they become a regular part of your diet, they can increase the production of free radicals in the body, which increases the likelihood of cancerous growth and other conditions. Craving fast foods and convenience snacks, such as cookies or chips, can be addictive over time, making an effort to switch to a healthier alternative challenging.

If you find ditching fast food difficult, consider healthier options on the menu, such as salads, baked potatoes, and soups. If you have the choice between deep-fried or baked, baked food may seem less appealing at first, though it can be delicious once you become accustomed to it.

Processed Meats

All processed meats should be avoided. This includes pre-packaged sliced deli meats, smoked meats, and anything that contains nitrates and carcinogens, both of which contribute to inflammation and some forms of cancer. Smoked meats can be enjoyed on occasion, though should be left off the menu as much as possible. For example, if you enjoy smoked salmon with capers as a treat now and again, this is acceptable. However, eating smoked hams, sausage, and other meats on a daily or even weekly basis should be avoided.

Pasta, White Bread, and Gluten

While not everyone may agree with ditching pasta, bread, and gluten entirely unless there is a condition that requires complete avoidance of gluten. Most foods in this category lack nutrition and are basically considered "filler" foods, which are often used as a supplement with meats and vegetables. White bread, for example, is void of nutrients, which makes whole-grain options a better choice overall. Pasta doesn't have to be skipped if you choose a low calorie or vegetable-based option. If moderation, most processed or refined foods are not harmful, though because they occupy a significant part of the traditional diet, they should be avoided as much as possible.

High-Fructose Corn Syrup

One of the most insidious foods that can contribute to a lot of health conditions is high-fructose corn syrup. It is often an item that is not clearly spelled out in the ingredients list, though many box bowls of cereal, baked goods, and mixes contain this ingredient. High-fructose corn syrup differs significantly from regular sugars and sweeteners, as it contains an extraordinarily high amount of concentrated sugar. When you eat a food product containing high fructose corn syrup, your body's ability to detect fullness may be impaired, which can cause overeating. Over a long period of time, the result is obesity and negative eating habits, as eating a high sugar diet is addictive and difficult to reverse, especially when your body's ability to detect fullness is not functioning properly.

Our body can only use so much glucose at a time, even when we are active and exercise often. This means that any residual amounts are stored in the body, resulting in extra weight. Coupled with overeating, this spells a disaster for weight gain and can contribute to the development of type 2 diabetes. High-fructose corn syrup also contributes to an increased risk of liver disease, stroke, and heart disease. While some forms of natural sweeteners in moderate amounts are harmless and may even contain some nutrients, high-fructose corn syrup is void of all nutrients, and the more you consume, the less room is left for more nutrient-rich foods that your body needs.

How can you avoid HFCS (high-fructose corn syrup)? There are some easy habits to avoiding this ingredient, including avoiding anything packaged in a box or carton that is sweetened. Not every label will include the exact wording "high-fructose corn syrup," which makes it challenging to detect in some products. For this reason, it's best to become acquainted with unnatural sweeteners that may lurk in packaged foods, or avoid them completely:

If you want to purchase hot cereals, choose raw oats on their own, and add your choice of sweeteners and ingredients, including cinnamon and maple syrup.

Avoid all sodas and artificially sweetened beverages. Some select drinks sweetened with low carb sweeteners or natural fruit extracts may be acceptable, though always review the ingredients carefully before consuming.

It's not just sweet foods and food products that contain HFCS. Among the products to watch for include canned tomato and pasta sauces, salad dressings, ice cream, bread, canned soups, various condiments and marinades, and many other products in cans or boxes.

Keep your focus on the outside aisles of the grocery store, where the vast majority of foods are fresh, unpackaged, and unprocessed. If you choose a dried fruit snack, check to make sure it's sundried, which means fewer additives were used in its preparation.

Avoid white and refined bread and baked goods, and instead choose whole grain and locally prepared goods, which list the ingredients. Bread containing flax seeds, caraway, and rye contain nutrients not found in white and refined goods.

Skip the fruit juices, and make your own freshly squeezed juice at home. Choose tea, skim milk, coffee, and water instead.

Avoid store-bought cookies, cakes, and pies, which are full of unnecessary sugars and additives that contribute to inflammation.

Many large-scale food product manufacturers have added some form of HFCS beginning over 40 years ago, which gives a thought to how much of an impact his additive has had on the increase of obesity and related illnesses over the past few decades. As we learn more about these products and additives, it's invaluable to making better decisions on how we select the foods and drinks we consume.

In general, avoiding as many processed foods as possible will provide a good foundation for reducing inflammation in your body and improving health overall. This may require a few slight adjustments to your current diet if you already make healthy choices during your shopping trips, or it may require a complete overhaul for a new and improved diet.

Chapter 2. What Foods to Eat and Which Ones to Avoid

Foods that are recommended to maintain proper levels of inflammation are the following ones:

Dark leafy greens, including spinach, kales;

Coldwater fish, including sardines, salmon;

All kinds of berries, such as cherries, blueberries;

Dark red grapes;

cinnamon and Turmeric;

Nutrition-dense vegetables, such as cauliflower, broccoli;

Extra virgin olive oil;

lentils, beans;

Green tea;

Red wine, in moderation;

☐ Coconut, Avocado;

Olives;

Walnuts, pine nuts, pistachios, and almonds;

Dark chocolate;

Herbs, Spices.

Gluten-free Grains - Grains like quinoa, millet, and oats are all suitable as they are a good source of vitamin A, B & C along with fiber.

Meat & Poultry – Fresh meat and fish are allowed in this diet as they are rich in protein and high in Omega 3.

Processed Meat – Processed meat falls in the category of the worst inflammatory food. Therefore, bacon, sausages and hot dogs are better to be avoided altogether. Due to the presence of compounds like advanced glycation products, they are bad for the body and can cause inflammation. Furthermore, they are linked to the occurrence of chronic diseases.

Grains – Grains made from wheat is another food that does not find any place in the anti-inflammatory diet. Because of the presence of gluten, wheat products can create situations that can trigger inflammation. Gluten has components that can affect negatively the lining of the digestive system. This condition called leaky gut can cause food particles and microbes to pass through without proper digestion.

Dairy – The evidence in the case of dairy products is not absolute. But it is becoming a food intolerance for many people. Therefore, it is better to avoid it if possible. Whether you can take dairy or not, depends on your individual tolerance.

Fats & Oil of a particular kind – Vegetable oil, trans-fat and canola oil can increase inflammation in the body. When these oils are heated at high temperatures, they can become inflammatory.

Foods high in sugar – Complete no-no products in the anti-inflammatory diet are high sugar ingredients. They can bring about higher levels of inflammatory.

Useful Tips & Directions to Get Started

As you are probably new to the diet, making significant changes from the start itself can be intimidating. In that case, you could start with smaller steps. Instead of changing your entire diet abruptly, you can try substituting one or two processed foods with fresh foods, for instance.

Once you have got a grasp, you can start making more changes.

If possible, always try to plan and prepare your meals ahead. The 14-day anti-inflammatory meal plan in this cookbook will be an excellent aid for you. When you have meals prepared ahead, you won't get tempted to seek outside food, which might be high in inflammatory substances. You are entirely aware of all the ingredients in it.

Drink more water.

Eat more whole plant foods as they can provide the anti-inflammatory nutrients which the body needs. Try eating rainbow style plant-based foods for optimal health. Focus on eating foods that are high in antioxidants and omega-3.

Chapter 3. Foods That Worsen Inflammation

Just as you want to be fully informed about foods that will alleviate and reduce inflammation, spend some time becoming familiar with the following inflammation-inducing foods. You'll want to be able to recognize these ingredients quickly to avoid them, especially when they're skillfully hidden by the manufacturer. If you intentionally avoid these inflammation-worsening foods for a few weeks, you may find your body doesn't crave them as much after all.

Gluten

Gluten, a protein in wheat that acts as a glue to help food maintain its shape and texture, seems to be the most talked about food compound in our country. Besides wheat, it's also in other grains like bulgur, farro, semolina, rye, spelt, and any flour made from these grains. For people with celiac disease—a genetic autoimmune disorder—the ingestion of gluten leads to damage in the small intestine. Even if you don't have celiac disease, gluten is still a difficult protein to digest, causing a wide array of symptoms from brain fog to joint pain. Anyone suffering from a chronic autoimmune disease will most likely benefit from eliminating gluten from their diet.

Gluten has been around since the dawn of time, so why has there been so much negativity about it in just this past decade? While ancient grains nourished our ancestors for thousands of years, it wasn't until this past century that modernized wheat varieties were created. One theory behind modern gluten intolerance stems from the use of new chemical pesticides while growing them.

Gluten can be hidden in everything from soy sauce to deli meat, so read the nutrition label for anything relating to wheat protein or gluten. Rather than replacing glutenous products like breads or pastas with gluten-free versions, simply add more nourishing anti-inflammatory foods to your plate (suggested in the pages of this book). Most gluten-free products contain lots of extra sugar and simple carbohydrates that aren't necessarily healthy for you either.

Dairy

While modern milk ads feature everyone from schoolteachers to Olympic athletes, dairy may not be as healthy as we've been led to believe. It's not milk's fault, however, but rather that of modernization and conventional processes thrust upon it.

Conventional dairy products often have added sugar and preservatives. They're also pasteurized at high heat, which means they're devoid of the natural enzymes that help the digestive tract properly break down milk's proteins. Pasteurized milk is a processed food. The healthier alternative for some people is organic, raw, cultured dairy, which is a whole and unadulterated food. Raw milk contains lactase, the enzyme required to digest lactose. Cultured dairy, like kefir and yogurt, contains beneficial bacteria that have partially digested the complete proteins found in the dairy, making it easier for humans to digest.

If you know you're sensitive to dairy, and because most conventional dairy sold today is pasteurized, consider trying cultured or raw dairy from a trusted organic source.

Soy

This controversial legume is a common allergen in the United States, yet it's widely enjoyed in many other countries. Part of the reason behind this controversy is that the majority of soy grown in the United States has been genetically modified, causing a wide variety of digestive problems in both animals and humans.

Soy contains high levels of an anti-nutrient called phytic acid, which prevents our bodies from absorbing other nutrients. The phytoestrogens found in soy have been linked to thyroid diseases like autoimmune disorders and cancer.

Fermenting soy can help neutralize some of the toxins found in it today, which is the way many other countries enjoy soy. Traditionally fermented soy sauce, miso, and tempeh are examples.

Corn

Like soy, corn is not inherently bad for you, but it's been treated in such a way over the past several decades that its chemical makeup has changed into a food that poses potentially serious health risks for consumers. Again, the majority of corn in the

United States is genetically modified and not organic, leading to compromised immune systems and the promotion of inflammation in our bodies.

If you were raised on a standard American diet, you've probably consumed lots of processed corn constituents like high fructose corn syrup and corn oil. When choosing to eat this grain, always choose a non-GMO organic from a trusted source.

Chapter 4. The Benefits of Following an Anti-Inflammatory Diet

Health and Lifestyle Benefits of Anti-Inflammatory Foods

Once you begin to implement foods with a high nutrient level and anti-inflammatory properties, you'll notice significant benefits often within one or two weeks. If you normally experience bloating and/or inflammation, you'll notice these symptoms will reduce and may disappear altogether. Over a longer time, you may notice the benefits of weight loss, improved energy, and a reduction in symptoms from a variety of health conditions. Following an anti-inflammatory diet should not be considered a temporary fix or a quick solution, but rather a long-term commitment that fits into your lifestyle.

How do Anti-Inflammatory Foods Work?

People who tend to follow a Mediterranean diet or consume plant-based foods only will naturally alleviate stress on the body and, therefore, prevent occurrences of inflammation. This also prevents the onset of diseases and conditions that develop as we age, and help improve how we function and focus as we grow older. Regular exercise, drinking plenty of water, and avoiding processed and sugary foods are also excellent ways to prevent disease and improve overall health.

Inflammation occurs as a response to our body's immune system, as a trigger when something isn't right. When we become inflamed, it's our body's way of trying to fight an infection or condition as a natural immune response. When this happens frequently and over a longer period of time, this process becomes a trigger for other diseases and conditions, such as Alzheimer's, depression, and diabetes. It can also lead to stroke and heart disease if left untreated. Many people take medication for the treatment of inflammation, though in the long-term, it only resolves the symptoms temporarily, while further damage is done within the body. For this reason, taking a more preventative approach to your health and bodily functions is key to living the best quality of life as possible.

Focus on Healthy Nuts and Seeds

Whether your focus is eating leaner meats, including fish and poultry, or consuming a plant-based diet, all can agree that nuts and seeds should become a mainstay in your way of eating, due to the sheer number of nutrients and minerals they contain, and in such small amounts. Just a small portion of nuts and/or seeds each day can replace some vitamin supplements while providing a nutritious snack. Making these small, but mighty foods a center of your diet is a good way to make the anti-inflammatory way of eating a successful lifestyle. To become more familiar with the benefits of nuts and seeds, research as much as possible, so that you know exactly which varieties to include, not just based on nutrients, but on taste and preference.

Almonds pack a good dose of protein, vitamin E, magnesium, and fiber. They contain very little carbohydrates and can improve cholesterol levels. In addition to having anti-inflammatory properties, almonds assist in weight loss and improving metabolism. They reduce blood pressure and improve blood sugar levels. This variety of nuts is ideal for people who have type 2 diabetes.

Walnuts are popular and used in a lot of desserts and as a salad topping. They contain a significant amount of healthy fats and fiber, making them ideal for weight loss and maintenance. Like almonds, they regulate blood sugar and improve metabolism, while preventing heart disease and other chronic conditions.

Pistachios are distinguishable by their greenish color once they are removed from their shells, and are often added to desserts, puddings, and drinks, including smoothies. They make a great topping to many dishes and can also be enjoyed as a snack, roasted or raw. Pistachios help improve heart health and provide a significant amount of healthy fats for overall bodily function. Blood pressure and glucose levels are lowered, and weight loss is also improved.

Pecans are one of the favorite nuts added to desserts, because of their pleasant texture and taste combination. They are often seen in butter tarts or pies, including ice creams and other treats. Pecans make a great snack on-the-go and provide a healthy dose of magnesium, which is essential for bone and muscle health. They are high in antioxidants and contain polyphenols, which are essentially antioxidants, which improve the quality of blood in the body while improving cholesterol levels.

While they are an expensive option compared to other nut varieties, macadamia nuts can be found in bulk stores and enjoyed in small portions, as well as in recipes.

Cashews are tasty raw or toasted, and often one of the most enjoyed snacks on their own. They are filling and make a great snack on their own, or mixed with other nuts and seeds. Metabolism and antioxidant performance have been noted in studies resulting from the consumption of cashews, as well as other nuts with similar nutrients. Cashews are high in fats and help regulate blood sugar and cholesterol.

Brazil nuts originate from the Amazon and contain selenium, a mineral that is also an antioxidant. Deficiency in selenium can lead to a number of diseases and conditions, which makes it vital for overall health and bodily function. It helps regulate your body's weight and metabolism.

Hazelnuts are one of the top options for spreads and additions to chocolate desserts and can be helpful in reducing the chances of heart disease. Hazelnuts are high in vitamin E and improve the blood vessel function in the body.

Peanuts are one of the most popular and common nuts used in recipes and everyday snacks. They are often found prepacked with salt and/or other flavors. For maximum benefits, peanuts are best consumed raw or lightly roasted, without any added salt or sugars. While they can trigger an allergic reaction for some people, they are generally safe for anyone who doesn't have any conditions impacted by peanuts. They are a good option for women who are pregnant, as regular consumption may reduce the likelihood of peanut allergies in children. This may also reduce the prevalence of childhood asthma as well. Peanut butter is another excellent option, provided no additional sugar, salt, or preservatives are added.

Seeds, like nuts, provide many health benefits and should be consumed as regularly as possible. Not all seeds may seem likely to become a part of your diet, though rotating them and trying a few varieties can give you a good idea of which ones you'd like to use more often. Some seeds are great as snacks on their own, such as sunflower or pumpkin seeds, while chia seeds, flax, and hemp seeds are used as ingredients in cereals, smoothies, and salads.

Chia seeds are small, tiny, black or reddish-brown seeds that have become more popular in recent years due to their high levels of nutrients. Just one small serving of chia seeds contains antioxidants, protein, calcium, magnesium, omega 3 and 6s, vitamin B1, and manganese. The increased production of ALA in the blood directly reduces the prevalence of inflammation, which is the effect of chia seeds in the body. Reducing blood sugar, improving type 2 diabetes symptoms, and reducing the likelihood of heart disease are among many other benefits of chia seeds. Fortunately, you don't have to eat large amounts to reap the benefits, though a regular, small portion of your daily routine will go a long way to improving your health overall.

Hemp seeds are an excellent source of protein and fatty acids. They contain important nutrients your body can't produce, which makes hemp an advantage to include in your diet. The quality of protein in hemp is considered high, which makes it a good option as a boost to smoothies. Some bulk stores and natural foods stores offer hemp protein powder as a supplement for vegan bodybuilding and as a powder to add to drinks, milkshakes, and smoothies. Hemp also helps improve skin health and can fight against eczema, as well as improving the moisture levels in the skin. Some people have shown a significant decrease in eczema symptoms after regular hemp use.

Flaxseeds are best to consume ground, rather than as whole seeds, in order to get the most out of their nutritious ingredients. High in antioxidants, fiber, and healthy fats, flaxseeds are often added to cereals, both hot and cold, to boost the nutrition value. They can also be added to smoothies like hemp and chia seeds. There are some studies that indicate possible prevention and treatment of tumors in some cases, which is promising for people who suffer from both benign and cancerous tumor growth.

Sesame seeds are often enjoyed as a topping on desserts, bagels, bread, or stir fry dishes. They are most popular lightly toasted and can blend in with many different dishes and flavors. Some studies indicate possible prevention of heart disease and cancer due to the high level of antioxidants. They also reduce inflammation, which provides relief from the effects of arthritis, including pain management. Consuming just a small portion of sesame seeds and/or powder each week can significantly reduce the inflammatory properties in the body. This can help improve and heal muscle stress and damage in athletes, which makes sesame powders and butter another great way to get a good dose of protein and healing properties for your body.

Pumpkin seeds are an excellent snack on-the-go, either raw or lightly roasted, without salt. They contain phytosterols, which contribute to lower blood sugar and the likelihood of breast cancer. Pumpkin seeds have shown positive results in the treatment and prevention of both bladder and kidney stones. Prevention occurs due to the seeds' ability to lower the amount of calcium in the urine, which contributes to the formation of stones. This also has the effect of improving prostate and urinary tract function, preventing disease and infection. Women may experience relief from menopause symptoms and lowering cholesterol.

Sunflower seeds are a tasty seed full of vitamins and healthy fats. There seems to be a significant amount of inflammation reduction, specifically in older adults, as well as reducing heart disease and other conditions associated with inflammation. While sunflower seeds are beneficial to anyone, they are especially helpful for aging adults over the age of 50, who are prone to more chronic conditions and health issues. Other studies show promising results in post-menopausal women who have type 2 diabetes, as well as lowering and regulating cholesterol levels.

In general, unless you experience adverse reactions or severe allergies to nuts or seeds, add as many varieties as possible into your diet as a regular staple. In fact, use nuts and seeds as the centerpiece of your diet and build your fruits, vegetables, and meat or vegan proteins around them. Making nuts and seeds the focus of your diet has many benefits in itself, for more reasons than health:

Nuts and seeds are portable and can be easily added to any dishes at home or on the go.

While some nuts and seeds are expensive, many can be purchased in bulk, making them easier to control in terms of portion and consumption. This will help you plan your budget around the foods you eat, to include portions and costs.

They are easy as a snack and when you are in a crunch for a meal. If you don't have time for breakfast in the morning or might skip a meal at the point in the day, a handful of nuts and/or seeds can fill the gap until you have the chance to enjoy a full meal.

Yogurt, oatmeal, salads, and smoothies are just some of the foods you can add nuts and seeds too, even when you don't have time to make them at home. For example, a take-out salad from the local restaurant or café near work can easily be topped with a few teaspoons of chia seeds, pistachios, and/or peanuts.

Chapter 5. What is an Anti-Inflammatory diet?

That when the body activates the inflammatory function it only does so to protect our body.

It was also previously explained that when this normal function of the organism is activated too often, regardless of the reason, it becomes harmful because it boosts oxidation, accelerates aging and helps the development of inflammatory diseases that can seriously impair our quality of life and well-being. They can even lead us to death in the most serious situations.

Everyone knows that food contributes to the body.

Some provide essential nutrients for its proper functioning while others only harm and sicken it.

Our health will depend on our diet and this is where the anti-inflammatory diet is of vital importance.

An anti-inflammatory diet is one whose main purpose is to prevent chronic inflammation or improve its symptoms when it has already been activated in the body.

It also serve to improve the symptoms of inflammations in general. That is to say, those people who suffer from inflammatory diseases or who are presenting symptoms of swelling caused by an injury can benefit a lot from it.

It is a diet that follows a number of principles that help us:

a.- Avoid hyperactivity of the immune system and promote its proper functioning.

b.- To purify our organism of toxins, which not only strengthens the immune system but also helps us to feel more cheerful, energetic, cheerful and healthy.

c.- Prevent certain harmful organisms such as bacteria or bad parasites from wreaking havoc on our health.

d.- Keeping ourselves healthy internally

In short, an anti-inflammatory diet is a diet rich in food that is effective in controlling abnormal inflammatory processes and providing us with all the nutrients our body needs to function optimally, free of inflammation.

It focuses on improving the immune system, digestive processes, intestinal flora, secretion of toxins and the like through food.

It is not, therefore, a diet to lose weight, although it is possible to lose weight through it because it deserve to reduce or avoid excessive consumption of fatty foods or rich in carbohydrates.

This is a diet to overcome inflammation, to ensure our health, to slow aging and to prevent a multitude of diseases arising from chronic inflammation.

Who should follow an anti-inflammatory diet?

Those who are going through the annoying symptoms of inflammation as a normal response of the body to an injury or harmful substance and wish to reduce its effects may follow an anti-inflammatory diet until there is improvement in swelling, redness, pain and numbness of the affected area.

Those who already suffer from inflammatory diseases should follow an anti-inflammatory diet to reduce their condition.

Those who show apparent signs of chronic inflammation (This topic was discussed earlier). That is, those who show signs of insomnia, irritability, exhaustion for no apparent reason or constant abdominal pain.

People who suffer from obesity because obesity keeps the immune system working actively and constantly.

Those who have smoked for too long and wish to detoxify their body.

And in general, everyone should follow an anti-inflammatory diet because it is a diet designed to maintain health, which should be a priority for everyone.

Principles of the anti-inflammatory diet:

In order to understand what the anti-inflammatory diet consists of, it is convenient to take into account the principles by which it is governed.

In this sense, an anti-inflammatory diet must comply with the following principles:

Avoid or reduce the intake of foods that enhance inflammation:

It will be impossible to fight inflammation if the organism is frequently bombarded with foods that activate the inflammatory reaction of the body and cause hyperactivity in the immune system.

That is why an effective anti-inflammatory diet will be one that avoids the inclusion in the diet of foods that enhance inflammation such as refined flours: (Bread flour, wheat flour, etc.), red meats, refined sugars, among others.

It is important to understand that although these foods are delicious, they are very harmful.

They may deceive our palate but they do not deceive our organism. Even less so with the immune system.

The immune system is simply activated when we consume these foods because it does not consider them food but harmful substances and that is what they really are. They bring virtually no benefit to our body or the few healthy nutrients they provide are overshadowed by the harmful ones.

Imagine how hard it must be for your immune system to be activated every time you eat a food that boosts inflammation. That makes it sick with time.

If you want to follow an anti-inflammatory diet and see real results you need to avoid the temptation to consume these foods.

Fortunately, foods that boost inflammation can easily be replaced by other healthy, nutrient-rich foods.

For example, the consumption of red meats, processed meats and sausages can be substituted by lean meats, hydrogen oils can be substituted by olive oil, bakery products and unhealthy snacks by fruits and vegetables or recipes that contain those ingredients...

Anti-inflammatory foods are also delicious. Give them a chance and you'll see.

In subsequent chapters, you'll come across a wealth of recipes that can help you once and for all to avoid the temptation to eat unhealthily.

Increase the consumption of foods rich in omega 3:

The omega 3 is an essential nutrient for our organism and in addition, it has demonstrated in diverse studies to have positive incidence in the improvement of inflammatory illnesses.

Therefore, an effective anti-inflammatory diet should include foods rich in omega 3 such as fish, lean meats and chia seeds.

What causes inflammation? Factors to consider that trigger of chronic inflammation can be very varied.

They are often related to each other, though.

It is important to know them because learning to detect them will make it easier for us to combat or avoid them.

These factors will be explained below:

Consuming unhealthy foods:

This is the factor that most often triggers chronic inflammation or at least, the one that most easily enhances its development.

The proper functioning of our body depends largely on our diet, which must be balanced and healthy.

The opposite only leads to our organism being altered.

We must not forget that we are what we eat.

If we eat well we will feel good and if we do it badly we will feel bad. That is a reality that we have to deal with day after day.

The right diet translates into more energy, more encouragement and a reduction in the likelihood of obesity, heart disease, diabetes and other health threats.

A diet lacking the nutrients necessary for our well-being and rich in fats and carbohydrates reduces our life expectancy and leads to obesity and other conditions, including chronic inflammation and all the underlying consequences of suffering it.

Intelligently the most convenient is to opt for the first option, right? For healthy eating?

Unfortunately junk food, refined flours and sugars, red meats, soft drinks and other harmful foods tempt us easily because of their pleasant taste.

It is easy to succumb to a bad diet but succumbing to unhealthy foods and eating too much of them will only lead to a host of diseases that we would really like to avoid.

It will also lead to inflammation.

As we already know, chronic inflammation is very harmful. Its presence in our body can make us seriously ill.

Many foods frequently consumed by most people trigger a wrong inflammatory reaction.

Our organism simply does not know these "foods" as nutrients and sees them as a threat. It rejects them.

The reality is that these foods are a poison to our body and enhance inflammation.

Here is a list of foods to avoid to prevent and fight inflammation:

Foods that cause inflammation:

Refined flours

Refined sugar

Red meat

Sausages

Hydrogen oils

Refreshments

Dairy products (Butter, margarine, too fatty cheeses)

Junk food

Alcohol

And in general, all processed foods !!

Reducing the consumption of these foods is vital in the fight against inflammation and its prevention.

Overweight:

Obesity and inflammation are related.

Chronic inflammation produces obesity and vice versa.

What is certain is that overweight generates inflammatory reactions in the intestine, abdomen and in the organism in general.

If we do not do something about it, the inflammatory reaction triggered by obesity will remain in our body longer than it should and there will appear the feared chronic inflammation.

This factor is closely related to the one explained above.

A diet based on flour, refined sugar and other foods harmful to health, such as those with excess fat or carbohydrates will lead us to obesity and consequently will cause us to suffer chronic inflammation.

This establishes the importance of a healthy diet to avoid inflammation and its ills.

Sedentary life:

This factor that triggers chronic inflammation is related to the previous ones.

Poor nutrition and a sedentary lifestyle will lead to the development of obesity and, as an underlying consequence, chronic inflammation will be present.

When you lead a sedentary lifestyle, your body doesn't work the right way because we don't help you oxygenate as you should. As a result, the immune system is likely to weaken and not function as well.

The weakened immune system will have to work harder to try to combat the harmful agents and external agents that can make our bodies sick.

This can undoubtedly lead to chronic inflammation.

Smoking:

For no one it is a secret that smoking is harmful to health and one of the leading causes of death around the world.

This bad habit damages to a great extent our lungs and promotes cancer in them and the appearance of inflammatory diseases such as gingivitis, rhinitis and the like. It also damages our dental health by contributing to weakened teeth.

Not to mention the bad breath that smokers have to deal with.

Some think that the negative effects of smoking are only those stated above. But they are wrong.

Smoking also enhances chronic inflammation.

When we smoke we let our lungs be bombarded by cigarette or tobacco smoke.

Our brain detects the presence of that smoke as an invasion and in response to it our immune system activates the inflammatory process.

If we smoke too often we will cause the body to trigger the process with the same frequency and sooner or later that causes the acute inflammation to become chronic.

Pollution:

Another of the triggers of chronic inflammation is pollution.

With pollution something similar happens to what happens with the action of smoking.

Exposure to pollutants often causes our immune system to activate to protect us from everything it considers invasive: smoke, bacteria that can adhere to us and are found in the trash, viruses that circulate in polluted air, among others.

Over time, that body's natural reaction will become chronic because it has been activated for too long or in a very repetitive manner.

Chapter 6. Inflammation FAQs

Q. What is the relation between the immune system and inflammation?

The immune system could be sufficiently described as the protector of the body from harm by invaders. Whenever it senses danger, be it in the form of an injury or disease-causing bacteria, the immune system sends out its resources to attack the invader. When the immune system responds in this way, actually sending out white blood cells to fight the problem, soreness occurs. The variable in this relationship is that while sometimes these protective tools are needed by the body, in other instances they are not needed.

Q. Does inflammation synonymously identify with infection?

No, these two words do not mean the same thing. They may be confusing because they are closely related. However, whilst infection identifies as the body's occupation by foreign invaders, inflammation identifies as the process through which the body strives to fend off the invading foreigners.

Q. Is there medication to treat inflammation?

Yes, there are forms of inflammation that can be treated with various medications. Such substances as steroids and non-steroidal anti-inflammatory drugs (NSAIDs) are able to treat inflammatory.

Q. Does inflammation influence other diseases?

Yes. Inflammation is associated with a broad range of diseases such as asthma, heart disease and cancer, among others.

Q. What is "shock?"

Shock is defined as a "circulatory collapse", a condition where the body's blood pressure is low, hindering sufficient and free flow of blood throughout the body. The symptoms of this condition include dilated pupils, dry mouth, irregular breathing, quickened pulse and increased perspiration.

Q. Are organic meats or eggs less inflammatory?

Poultry and meat that have been raised on organic feed, free of antibiotics or hormones could be more nutritious. The challenge is a lack of nutritional data on these foods and the variety between the producers.

Q. Does a person who does not suffer from allergies or arthritis need to worry about inflammation?

Every person should worry about inflammation because it can happen to anyone, for a number of reasons. Inflammation can cause obvious symptoms such as asthma and joint pain.

Q. How does one know how to tell which foods are inflammatory?

It is complicated to distinguish foods that are inflammatory from foods that are anti-inflammatory. This is because some foods actually come with a combination of anti-inflammatory and inflammatory effects. The best motto is to research, practice and experiment!

As we already discussed, there are numerous benefits in following the Anti-inflammatory diet. Professionals and experts suggest following the Anti-inflammatory diet without giving it a second thought. However, before you start, there are a few rules that you must follow, which will be discussed below:

Your primary focus should be on plant-based foods, including vegetables, fruits, whole grains, nuts, and legumes.

You must replace butter with olive oil or other healthy oils.

You must opt for spices and herbs instead of salt.

You must add poultry and fish to your diet at least two times a week.

You must limit red meat consumption, and eat only on special occasions or a few times a month.

You must drink a lot of water and steer clear of unhealthy drinks. You can enjoy red wine in moderation.

You must engage in exercise.

Eat with your family and friends.

All these factors are essential because together, they will support your overall health. For example, eating with friends and family might not be outlined as a rule in any other diets, but in the Anti-inflammatory diet it is. Why do you think it is essential to dine with friends or family? Eating with family and friends will allow you to enjoy the food even more. You can test this out and see for yourself.

Traditionally, the Anti-inflammatory diet consists of pasta, rice, fruits, and vegetables. If you study the lifestyle of people in the Mediterranean region, you will understand their eating habits and why these foods are included in the diet. Even the grains in that region are whole grains and therefore have less trans fats. Bread is especially considered a vital part of this diet. When eating bread, it is essential not to apply margarine or butter to it because they contain trans fats, which is what we're trying to stay away from. Instead, you should coat the bread with olive oil. Nuts are an integral part of the diet too. You don't have to worry about the high calories in nuts because they are not saturated fats. When eating nuts, you shouldn't exceed the limit; simply try to limit your intake to a specified amount (maybe a handful of nuts) per day. You cannot substitute regular nuts for other nuts such as honey-roasted, salted, and candied. If you do, they will no longer fall under the allowed list of foods in the Anti-inflammatory diet.

As you already know, the Anti-inflammatory diet isn't entirely focused on fat consumption. Both hydrogenated oils and saturated fats are not encouraged in the Anti-inflammatory diet because they can lead to the development of heart disease.

Olive oil is considered the best type of oil that can be consumed in the Anti-inflammatory diet, as it has monounsaturated fats; therefore, it reduces the levels of LDL cholesterol. Both virgin and extra-virgin olive oils are processed in the lowest form. They contain antioxidants which are needed for the body. Linolenic acid is found in polyunsaturated fats and monounsaturated fats. Omega-3 fatty acids help to reduce triglycerides and blood clotting. They will enhance the health of the blood vessels as well. You can eat fish regularly, as well as fatty fish including lake trout, sardines, mackerel, salmon, and tuna, as they are enriched with omega-3 fatty acids.

Alcohol is not recommended by the Anti-inflammatory diet. There has been an ongoing debate about whether or not alcohol consumption should be permitted in this diet. Some professionals don't allow the consumption of alcohol, however, wine consumption is allowed if the dieter only moderately consumes it.

Women are allowed to consume around 148 milliliters of wine, which is five ounces per day. Men (under the age of 65) are allowed to consume around 296 milliliters, which adds up to ten ounces per day. If you are someone who has little control over consumption of wine or alcohol, it's best to stay away from it altogether. This way, you will be able to control your cravings, and opt for something else instead.

It can be tough to get started on this type of diet, even if you know what to eat and what to avoid. But if you can find a way to create a specialized meal plan, you will be able to move forward with ease.

Below I've outlined a few steps that you should follow if you want to get started with this type of diet.

Find solutions for snacks: at some point, you will want to grab a quick snack, so what kind of snacks are you allowed to have? Some snacks you're allowed to eat are cashews, almonds, walnuts, pistachios, and even non hydrogenated peanut butter. You can easily prepare these snacks in an instant. Just remember to keep your snacking habits at a healthy level!

Have more fruits and veggies: in the past, vegetables may not have been your favorite, but if they can improve your overall health, you should add them to your diet plan. Try to include whole grains, fruits, and veggies as much as possible. Your meals should have a high percentage of plant-based foods. It's best to have around 7-10 servings of fruits or vegetables per day. You should also consider whole-grain products such as pasta and rice.

Ditch the butter: Butter is not necessary if you have extra virgin olive oil because it serve the same purpose as butter would.

Add fish: Add tuna, mackerel, trout, and other healthy choices of fish to your diet. If you are interested in fried fish, you should first make sure you use the right type of oil, such as olive oil or canola oil.

Opt for spices and herbs: If you have been using salt, it is time to switch to spices and herbs because they promote health and are delicious.

Consider low-fat diary: Opt for products that are low in fat like fat-free cheese, yogurt, and skim milk. Stay away from dairy products that have a high fat percentage.

The above list is important, and you should familiarize yourself with it before starting your journey on the Anti-inflammatory diet. Below, I've gone into more detail about the foods you can and cannot have with this diet.

Chapter 7. Breakfast Recipes

Oats with Berries

Preparation Time: 10 Minutes

Cooking Preparation Time: 30 Minutes

Servings: 4

Ingredients:

1 cup Steel Cut Oats

Dash of Salt

3 cups Water

For toppings:

½ cup Berries of your choice

¼ cup Nuts or Seeds of your choice like Almonds or Hemp Seeds

Method of Preparation:

To begin with, place the oats in a small saucepan and heat it over medium-high heat.

Now, toast it for 3 minutes while stirring the pan frequently.

Next, pour water to the saucepan and mix well.

Allow the mixture to boil. Lower the heat.

Allow it to cook for 23 to 25 minutes or until the oats are cooked and tender.

Once done cooking, transfer the mixture to the serving bowl and top it with the berries and seeds.

Serve it warm or cold.

Tip: If you desire, you can add sweeteners like maple syrup or coconut sugar or stevia to it.

Nutrition:

Calories: 118Kcal

Proteins: 4.1g

Carbohydrates: 16.5g

Fat: 4.4g

Spinach Avocado Smoothie

Preparation Time: 5 Minutes

Cooking Preparation Time: 5 Minutes

Servings: 1

Ingredients:

¼ of 1 Avocado

1 cup Plain Yoghurt, non-fat

2 tbsp. Water

1 cup Spinach, fresh

1 tsp. Honey

1 Banana, frozen

Method of Preparation:

Start by blending all the ingredients needed to make the smoothie in a high-speed blender for 2 to 3 minutes or until you get a smooth and creamy mixture.

Next, transfer the mixture to a serving glass.

Serve and enjoy.

Tip: If you don't prefer to use yogurt, you can use unsweetened almond milk.

Nutrition:

Calories: 357Kcal

Proteins: 17.7g

Carbohydrates: 57.8g

Fat: 8.2g

Golden Milk

Preparation Time: 5 Minutes

Cooking Preparation Time: 5 Minutes

Servings: 2

Ingredients:

1 tbsp. Coconut Oil

1 ½ cups Coconut Milk, light

Pinch of Pepper

1 ½ cups Almond Milk, unsweetened

¼ tsp. Ginger, grated

1 ½ tsp. Turmeric, grounded

¼ tsp. Cinnamon, grounded

Sweetener of your choice, as needed

Method of Preparation:

To make this healthy beverage, you need to place all the ingredients in a medium-sized saucepan and mix it well.

After that, heat it over medium heat for 3 to 4 minutes or until it is hot but not boiling. Stir continuously.

Taste for seasoning. Add more sweetener or spice as required by you.

Finally, transfer the milk to the serving glass and enjoy it.

Tip: Instead of cinnamon powder, you can also use the cinnamon stick, which can be discarded at the end if you prefer a much more intense flavour.

Nutrition:

Calories: 205Kcal

Proteins: 3.2g

Carbohydrates: 8.9g

Fat: 19.5g

Granola

Preparation Time: 10 Minutes

Cooking Preparation Time: 60 Minutes

Servings: 2

Ingredients:

½ cup Flax Seeds, grounded

1 cup Almonds, whole & raw

½ cup Ginger, grated

1 cup Pumpkin Seeds, raw

½ tsp. Salt

1 cup Shredded Coconut, unsweetened

¾ cup Water

1 cup Oat Bran

½ cup Coconut Oil, melted

1 cup Dried Cherries, pitted

4 tsp. Turmeric Powder

Method of Preparation:

First, preheat the oven to 300 ° F.

Next, combine dried cherries, almonds, grounded flax, pumpkin seeds, coconut, salt, and turmeric in a large mixing bowl until mixed well.

After that, mix ginger, coconut oil, and water in the blender and blend for 30 to 40 seconds or until well incorporated.

Now, spoon in the coconut oil mixture to the nut mixture. Mix well.

Then, transfer the mixture to a parchment paper-lined baking sheet and spread it across evenly.

Bake for 50 to 60 minutes while checking on it once or twice.

Allow it to cool completely and enjoy it.

Tip: Substitute dried cherries with raisins if preferred.

Nutrition:

Calories: 225Kcal

Proteins: 6g

Carbohydrates: 18g

Fat: 16g

Overnight Coconut Chia Oats

Preparation Time: 10 Minutes

Cooking Preparation Time: 60 Minutes

Servings: 1 to 2

Ingredients:

½ cup Coconut Milk, unsweetened

2 tsp. Chia Seeds

1 ½ cups Old Fashioned Oats, whole grain

½ tsp. Cinnamon, grounded

1 cup Almond Milk, unsweetened

½ tsp. Cinnamon, grounded

2 tsp. Date Syrup

½ tsp. Black Pepper, grounded

1 tsp. Turmeric, grounded

Method of Preparation:

To start with, keep the oats in the mason jar.

After that, mix the rest of the ingredients in a medium bowl until combined well.

Then, pour the mixture to the jars and stir well.

Now, close the jar and place it in the refrigerator overnight.

In the morning, stir the mixture and then enjoy it.

Tip: You can top it with toasted nuts or berries.

Nutrition:

Calories: 335Kcal

Proteins: 8g

Carbohydrates: 34.1g

Fat: 19.9g

Scrambled Eggs

Preparation Time: 10 Minutes

Cooking Preparation Time: 20 Minutes

Servings: 5

Ingredients:

1 tsp. Turmeric Powder

10 Eggs, large & preferably farm-raised

¼ tsp. Black Pepper

½ cup Almond Milk, unsweetened

¼ tsp. Cumin

¼ tsp. Sea Salt

Method of Preparation:

For making this easy breakfast, preheat the oven to 350 ° F.

After that, combine milk, cumin, eggs, pepper, salt, and turmeric in a large mixing bowl with a whisker.

Next, pour the egg batter to a greased glass casserole dish.

Then, bake for 11 to 12 minutes or until the eggs have started to set.

Once the time is up, remove the dish from the oven and stir it once with a wooden spatula.

Return the dish to the oven. Bake for further 8 minutes or until the egg is set.

Top it with cilantro, if preferred.

Tip: You can add your favourite anti-inflammatory veggies into it for more flavour and nutrition.

Nutrition:

Calories: 149Kcal

Proteins: 12.8g

Carbohydrates: 1.3g

Fat: 3.1g

Blueberry Hemp Seed Smoothie

Preparation Time: 10 Minutes

Cooking Preparation Time: 5 Minutes

Servings: 1

Ingredients:

1 ¼ cup Blueberries, frozen

1 ¼ cup Plant-Based Milk of your choice

2 tbsp. Hemp Seeds

1 tsp. Spirulina

1 scoop of Protein Powder

Method of Preparation:

First, place all the ingredients needed to make the smoothie in a high-speed blender and blend them for 2 minutes or until smooth.

Transfer the mixture to a serving glass and enjoy it.

Tip: Instead of blueberries, you can use any berries of your choice.

Nutrition:

Calories: 493Kcal

Proteins: 37.8g

Carbohydrates: 46.3g

Fat: 19.6g

Quinoa Porridge

Preparation Time: 10 Minutes

Cooking Preparation Time: 5 Minutes

Servings: 1

Ingredients:

½ cup Quinoa, cooked

¼ cup Almonds, chopped

1/4 cup Sunflower Seeds

1 tbsp. Maple Syrup

2 tbsp. Dates, finely chopped

¼ cup Almond Milk

Pinch of Cinnamon

Method of Preparation:

To begin with, combine all the ingredients in a large saucepan over medium heat.

Cook for 7 to 8 minutes or until the porridge is cooked and reaches your preferred consistency.

Serve it hot or warm.

Tip: To up the nutritional content, you can even add flax seeds or chia seeds.

Nutrition:

Calories: 493Kcal

Proteins: 37.8g

Carbohydrates: 46.3g

Fat: 19.6g

Spiced Morning Chia Pudding

Preparation Time: 10 Minutes

Cooking Preparation Time: 5 Minutes

Servings: 1

Ingredients:

½ tsp. Cinnamon

1 ½ cups Cashew Milk

1/8 tsp. Cardamom, grounded

1/3 cup Chia Seeds

1/8 tsp. Cloves, grounded

2 tbsp. Maple Syrup

1 tsp. Turmeric

Method of Preparation:

To begin with, combine all the ingredients in a medium bowl until well mixed.

Next, spoon the mixture into a container and allow it to sit overnight.

In the morning, transfer to a cup and serve with toppings of your choice.

Tip: You can top it with toppings of your choice like coconut flakes or seeds etc.

Nutrition:

Calories: 237Kcal

Proteins: 8.1g

Carbohydrates: 28.9g

Fat: 8.1g

Green Smoothie

Preparation Time: 10 Minutes

Cooking Preparation Time: 10 Minutes

Servings: 1

Ingredients:

2 cups Kale

1 tbsp. Chia Seeds

½ of 1 Banana, medium

1 cup Pineapple Chunks, frozen

¼ tsp. Turmeric

1 cup Green Tea, brewed & cooled

1 scoop of Protein Powder

2/3 cup Cucumber, cut into chunks

3 Mint Leaves

½ cup Mango, cut into chunks

½-inch Ginger, sliced

Ice Cubes, if needed

Method of Preparation:

To start with, place all the ingredients in a high-speed blender, excluding the chia seeds and blend them for 2 to 3 minutes or until smooth.

Next, put in the chia seeds and blend them for a further 1 minute.

Finally, transfer to a serving glass and enjoy it.

Tip: You can substitute kale with spinach if desired.

Nutrition:

Calories: 445Kcal

Proteins: 31.9g

Carbohydrates: 73.7g

Fat: 7.2g

Oatmeal Pancakes

Preparation Time: 10 Minutes

Cooking Preparation Time: 25 Minutes

Servings: 2

Ingredients:

1 ½ cups Rolled Oats, whole-grain

2 Eggs, large & pastured

2 tsp. Baking Powder

1 Banana, ripe

2 tbsp. Water

¼ cup Maple Syrup

1 tsp. Vanilla Extract

2 tbsp. Extra Virgin Olive Oil

Method of Preparation:

To make this delicious breakfast dish, you need to first blend all the ingredients in a high-speed blender for a minute or two or until you get a smooth batter. Tip: To blend easily, pour egg, banana, and all other liquid ingredients first and finally add oats at the end.

Now, take a large skillet and heat it over medium-low heat.

Once the skillet is hot, ¼ cup of the batter into it and cook it for 3 to 4 minutes per side or until bubbles start appearing in the middle portion.

Turn the pancake and cook the other side also.

Serve warm.

Tip: You can pair it with maple syrup and fruits.

Nutrition:

Calories: 201Kcal

Proteins: 5g

Carbohydrates: 28g

Fat: 8g

Anti-inflammatory Porridge

Preparation Time: 10 Minutes

Cooking Preparation Time: 25 Minutes

Servings: 2

Ingredients:

¾ cup Almond Milk, unsweetened

2 tbsp. Hemp Seeds

2 tbsp. Chia Seeds, whole

¼ cup Walnuts, halved

¼ cup Almond Butter

¼ cup Coconut Flakes, unsweetened & toasted

¼ cup Coconut Milk

½ tsp. Turmeric Powder

Dash of Black Pepper, grounded, as needed

½ tsp. Cinnamon

1 tbsp. Extra Virgin Olive Oil

Method of Preparation:

To start with, heat a large saucepan over medium heat.

To this, put in the hemp seeds, flaked coconut, and chopped walnuts.

Roast for 2 minutes or until toasted.

Once the coconut-seed mixture is roasted, transfer to a bowl and set it aside.

Then, heat almond milk and coconut milk in a wide saucepan over medium heat.

Once it becomes hot but not boiling, remove from the heat. Stir in almond butter and coconut oil to it. Mix.

Now, add chia seeds, pepper powder, turmeric powder, and salt to the milk. Combine.

Keep it aside for 5 minutes and then add half of the roasted coconut mixture. Mix.

Finally, transfer to a serving bowl and top with the remaining coconut mixture.

Serve immediately.

Tip: If possible, try adding bee pollen for enhanced taste.

Nutrition:

Calories: 575Kcal

Proteins: 14.8g

Carbohydrates: 6g

Fat: 50.2g

Cherry Smoothie

Preparation Time: 5 Minutes

Cooking Preparation Time: 2 Minutes

Servings: 1

Ingredients:

½ cup Cherries, pitted & frozen

½ of 1 Banana, frozen

10 oz. Almond Milk, unsweetened

1 tbsp. Almonds

1 Beet, small & quartered

Method of Preparation:

To make this delightful smoothie, you need to blend all the ingredients in a high-speed blender for 3 minutes or until smooth.

Pour to a serving glass and enjoy it.

Tip: If you wish, you can add one more beet to it.

Nutrition:

Calories: 208Kcal

Proteins: 5.2g

Carbohydrates: 34.4g

Fat: 7.1g

Gingerbread Oatmeal

Preparation Time: 10 Minutes

Cooking Preparation Time: 30 Minutes

Servings: 4

Ingredients:

¼ tsp. Cardamom, grounded

4 cups Water

¼ tsp. Allspice

1 cup Steel Cut Oats

1/8 tsp. Nutmeg

1 ½ tbsp. Cinnamon, grounded

¼ tsp. Ginger, grounded

¼ tsp. Coriander, grounded

Maple Syrup, if desired

¼ tsp. Cloves

Method of Preparation:

First, place all the ingredients in a large saucepan over medium-high heat and stir well.

Next, cook them for 6 to 7 minutes or until cooked.

Once finished, add the maple syrup.

Top it with dried fruits of your choice if desired.

Serve it hot or cold.

Tip: Avoid those spices which you don't prefer.

Nutrition:

Calories: 175Kcal

Proteins: 6g

Carbohydrates: 32g

Fat: 32g

Roasted Almonds

Servings: 32

Preparation Time: 5 minutes

Cooking Preparation Time: 10 minutes

Ingredients:

2 cups whole almonds

1 tablespoon chili powder

½ teaspoon ground cinnamon

½ teaspoon ground cumin

½ teaspoon ground coriander

Salt and freshly ground black pepper, to taste

1 tablespoon extra-virgin organic olive oil

Directions:

Preheat the oven to 350 degrees F. Line a baking dish with a parchment paper.

In a bowl, add all ingredients and toss to coat well.

Transfer the almond mixture into prepared baking dish in a single layer.

Roast for around 10 minutes, flipping twice inside the middle way.

Remove from oven and make aside to cool down the completely before serving.

You can preserve these roasted almonds in airtight jar.

Nutrition:

Calories: 62, Fat: 5g, Carbohydrates: 12g, Protein: 2g, Fiber 6g

Roasted Pumpkin Seeds

Servings: 4

Preparation Time: 10 minutes

Cooking Preparation Time: 20 minutes

Ingredients:

1 cup pumpkin seeds, washed and dried

2 teaspoons garam masala

1/3 teaspoon red chili powder

¼ teaspoon ground turmeric

Salt, to taste

3 tablespoons coconut oil, meted

½ tablespoon fresh lemon juice

Directions:

Preheat the oven to 350 degrees F.

In a bowl, add all ingredients except lemon juice and toss to coat well.

Transfer the almond mixture right into a baking sheet.

Roast approximately twenty or so minutes, flipping occasionally.

Remove from oven and make aside to cool completely before serving.

Drizzle with freshly squeezed lemon juice and serve.

Nutrition:

Calories: 136 Fat: 4g, Carbohydrates: 15g, Fiber: 9g, Protein: 25g

Roasted Chickpeas

Servings: 8-10

Preparation Time: 10 minutes

Cooking Preparation Time: one hour

Ingredients:

3 cups canned chickpeas, rinsed and dried

2 tablespoons nutritional yeast

1 tablespoon ground turmeric

½ teaspoon garlic powder

Pinch of cayenne pepper.

Salt and freshly ground black pepper, to taste

2 tablespoons extra-virgin organic olive oil

Directions:

Preheat the oven to 400 degrees F.

In a bowl, add all ingredients except freshly squeezed lemon juice and toss to coat well.

Transfer the almond mixture right into a baking sheet.

Roast for around 1 hour, flipping after every 15 minutes.

Remove from oven and keep aside for cooling completely before serving.

Drizzle with freshly squeezed lemon juice and serve.

Nutrition:

Calories: 190 Fat: 5g, Carbohydrates: 16g, Fiber: 7g, Protein: 12g

Spiced Popcorn

Servings: 2-3

Preparation Time: 5 minutes

Cooking Preparation Time: 2 minutes

Ingredients:

3 tablespoons coconut oil

½ cup popping corn

1 tbsp. olive oil

1 teaspoon ground turmeric

¼ teaspoon garlic powder

Salt, to taste

Directions:

In a pan, melt coconut oil on medium-high heat.

Add popping corn and cover the pan tightly.

Cook, shaking the pan occasionally for around 1-2 minutes or till corn kernels begin to pop.

Remove from heat and transfer right into a large heatproof bowl.

Add essential olive oil and spices and mix well.

Serve immediately

Nutrition:

Calories: 200, Fat: 4g, Carbohydrates: 12g, Fiber: 1g, Protein: 6g

Cucumber Bites

Servings: 4

Preparation Time: 15 minutes

Ingredients:

½ cup prepared hummus

2 teaspoons nutritional yeast

¼-½ teaspoon ground turmeric

Pinch of red pepper cayenne

Pinch of salt

1 cucumber, cut diagonally into ¼-½-inch thick slices

1 teaspoon black sesame seeds

Fresh mint leaves, for garnishing

Directions:

In a bowl, mix together hummus, turmeric, cayenne and salt.

Transfer the hummus mixture in the pastry bag and pipe on each cucumber slice.

Serve while using garnishing of sesame seeds and mint leaves.

Nutrition:

Calories: 203 Fat: 4g, Carbohydrates: 20g, Fiber: 3g, Protein: 8g

Spinach Fritters

Servings: 2-3

Preparation Time: 15 minutes

Cooking Preparation Time: 5 minutes

Ingredients:

2 cups chickpea flour

¾ teaspoons white sesame seeds

½ teaspoon garam masala powder

½ teaspoon red chili powder

¼ teaspoon ground cumin

2 pinches of baking soda

Salt, to taste

1 cup water

12-14 fresh spinach leaves

Olive oil, for frying

Directions:

In a sizable bowl, add all ingredients except spinach and oil and mix till an easy mixture forms.

In a sizable skillet, heat oil on medium heat.

Dip each spinach leaf in chickpea flour mixture evenly and place in the hot oil in batches.

Cook, flipping occasionally for about 3-5 minutes or till golden brown from each side.

Transfer the fritters onto paper towel lined plate.

Nutrition:

Calories: 211 Fat: 2g, Carbohydrates: 13g, Fiber: 11g, Protein: 9g

Crispy Chicken Fingers

Servings: 4-6

Preparation Time: 15 minutes

Cooking Preparation Time: 18 minutes

Ingredients:

2/3 cup almond meal

½ teaspoon ground turmeric

½ teaspoon red pepper cayenne

½ teaspoon paprika

½ teaspoon garlic powder

Salt and freshly ground black pepper, to taste

1 egg

1-pound skinless, boneless chicken breasts, cut into strips

Directions:

Preheat the oven to 375 degrees F. Line a substantial baking sheet with parchment paper.

In a shallow dish, beat the egg.

In another shallow dish, mix together almond meal and spices.

Coat each chicken strip with egg after which roll into spice mixture evenly.

Arrange the chicken strips onto prepared baking sheet in the single layer.

Bake for approximately 16-18 minutes.

Nutrition:

Calories: 236 Fat: 10g, Carbohydrates: 26g, Fiber: 5g, Protein: 37g

Chicken Popcorn

Servings: 2

Preparation Time: 15 minutes

Cooking Preparation Time: 25 minutes

Ingredients:

½ pound chicken thigh, cut into bite-sized pieces

7-ounce coconut milk

1-2 teaspoons ground turmeric

Salt and freshly ground black pepper, to taste

2 tablespoons coconut flour

3 tablespoons desiccated coconut

1 tablespoon coconut oil, melted

Directions:

In a large bowl, mix together chicken, coconut milk, turmeric, salt and black pepper.

Cover and refrigerate to marinate for overnight.

Preheat the oven to 390 degrees F.

In a shallow dish, mix together coconut flour and desiccated coconut.

Coat the chicken pieces in coconut mixture evenly.

Arrange chicken piece right into a baking sheet.

Drizzle with oil evenly.

Bake for around 20-25 minutes.

Nutrition:

Calories: 365 Fat: 8g, Carbohydrates: 25g, Fiber: 6g, Protein: 34g

Tuna & Sweet Potato Croquettes

Servings: 8

Preparation Time: 15 minutes

Cooking Preparation Time: 12 minutes

Ingredients:

1 tablespoon coconut oil

½ of large onion, chopped

1 (1-inchpiece fresh ginger, minced

3 garlic cloves, minced

1 Serrano pepper, seeded and minced

½ teaspoon ground coriander

¼ teaspoon ground turmeric

¼ teaspoon red chili powder

¼ teaspoon garam masala

Salt and freshly ground black pepper, to taste

2 (5-ouncecans tuna

1 cup cooked sweet potato, peeled and mashed

1 egg

¼ cup tapioca flour

¼ cup almond flour

Olive oil, as required

Directions:

In a frying pan, melt coconut oil on medium heat.

Add onion, ginger, garlic and Serrano pepper and sauté for approximately 5-6 minutes.

Stir in spices and sauté approximately 1 minute more.

Transfer the onion mixture in a bowl.

Add tuna and sweet potato and mix till well combined.

Make equal sized oblong shaped patties in the mixture.

Arrange the croquettes inside a baking sheet in a very single layer and refrigerate for overnight.

In a shallow dish, beat the egg.

In another shallow dish mix together both flours.

In a big skillet, heat the enough oil.

Add croquettes in batches and shallow fry for around 2-3 minutes per side.

Nutrition:

Calories: 404 Fat: 9g, Carbohydrates: 20g, Fiber: 4g, Protein: 30g

Quinoa & Veggie Croquettes

Servings: 12-15

Preparation Time: 15 minutes

Cooking Preparation Time: 9 minutes

Ingredients:

1 tbsp. essential olive oil

½ cup frozen peas, thawed

2 minced garlic cloves

1 cup cooked quinoa

2 large boiled potatoes, peeled and mashed

¼ cup fresh cilantro leaves, chopped

2 teaspoons ground cumin

1 teaspoon garam masala

¼ teaspoon ground turmeric

Salt and freshly ground black pepper, to taste

Olive oil, for frying

Directions:

In a frying pan, heat oil on medium heat.

Add peas and garlic and sauté for about 1 minute.

Transfer the pea mixture into a large bowl.

Add remaining ingredients and mix till well combined.

Make equal sized oblong shaped patties from your mixture.

In a large skillet, heat oil on medium-high heat.

Add croquettes and fry for about 4 minutes per side.

Nutrition:

Calories: 367 Fat: 6g, Carbohydrates: 17g, Fiber: 5g, Protein: 22g

Turkey Burgers

Servings: 5

Preparation Time: 15 minutes

Cooking Preparation Time: 8 minutes

Ingredients:

1 ripe pear, peeled, cored and chopped roughly

1-pound lean ground turkey

1 teaspoon fresh ginger, grated finely

2 minced garlic cloves

1 teaspoon fresh rosemary, minced

1 teaspoon fresh sage, minced

Salt and freshly ground black pepper, to taste

1-2 tablespoons coconut oil

Directions:

In a blender, add pear and pulse till smooth.

Transfer the pear mixture in a large bowl with remaining ingredients except oil and mix till well combined.

Make small equal sized 10 patties from mixture.

In a heavy-bottomed frying pan, heat oil on medium heat.

Add the patties and cook for around 4-5 minutes.

Flip the inside and cook for approximately 2-3 minutes.

Nutrition:

Calories: 477 Fat: 15g, Carbohydrates: 26g, Fiber: 11g, Protein: 35g

Lamb Burgers

Servings: 6

Preparation Time: 15 minutes

Cooking Preparation Time: 8 minutes

Ingredients:

1½ pound ground lamb

3 scallions, chopped

1 tablespoon fresh ginger, grated finely

Salt and freshly ground black pepper, to taste

Directions:

Preheat the grill to medium heat. Grease the grill gate.

In a bowl, add all ingredients and mix till well combined.

Make equal sized small patties from your mixture.

Grill the patties for about 4 minutes from either side.

Nutrition:

Calories: 465 Fat: 10g, Carbohydrates: 23g, Fiber: 7g, Protein: 31g

Salmon Burgers

Servings: 3

Preparation Time: 15 minutes

Cooking Preparation Time: 8 minutes

Ingredients:

1 (6-ouncecan skinless, boneless salon, drained

1 celery rib, chopped

½ of medium onion, chopped

2 large eggs

1 tablespoon plus 1 teaspoon coconut flour

1 tablespoon dried dill, crushed

1 teaspoon lemon pepper

Salt and freshly ground black pepper, to taste

3 tablespoons coconut oil

Directions:

In a substantial bowl, add salmon and which has a fork, break it into small pieces.

Add remaining ingredients except oil and mix till well combined.

Make 6 equal sized small patties from mixture.

In a substantial skillet, melt coconut oil on medium-high heat.

Cook the patties for around 3-4 minutes per side.

Nutrition:

Calories: 393 Fat: 12g, Carbohydrates: 19g, Fiber: 5g, Protein: 24g

Quinoa & Beans Burgers

Servings: 12

Preparation Time: 15 minutes

Cooking Preparation Time: 55 minutes

Ingredients:

½ cup dry quinoa

1½ cups water

1 cup cooked corn kernels

1 (15-ouncecan black beans, rinsed and drained

1 small boiled potato, peeled

1 small onion, chopped

½ teaspoon fresh ginger, grated finely

1 teaspoon garlic, minced

½ cup fresh cilantro, chopped

1 teaspoon flax meal

1 teaspoon ground cumin

1 teaspoon paprika

1 teaspoon chili flakes

½ teaspoon ground turmeric

Salt and freshly ground black pepper, to taste

Directions:

In a pan, add water and quinoa on high heat and provide to a boil.

Reduce heat to medium and simmer for around 15-twenty or so minutes.

Drain excess water.

Preheat the oven to 375 degrees F. Line a sizable baking sheet with parchment paper.

In a sizable bowl, add quinoa and remaining ingredients.

With a fork, mix till well combined.

Make equal sized patties from mixture.

Arrange the patties onto prepared baking sheet in the single layer.

Bake for around 20-25 minutes.

Carefully, alter the side and cook for about 8-10 minutes.

Nutrition:

Calories: 400 Fat: 9g, Carbohydrates: 27g, Fiber: 12g, Protein: 38g

Veggie Balls

Servings: 5-6

Preparation Time: 15 minutes

Cooking Preparation Time: 25 minutes

Ingredients:

2 medium sweet potatoes, peeled and cubed into ½-inch size

2 tablespoons coconut milk

1 cup fresh kale leaves, trimmed and chopped

1 medium shallot, chopped finely

1 teaspoon ground cumin

½ teaspoon granulated garlic

¼ teaspoon ground turmeric

Salt and freshly ground black pepper, to taste

Ground flax seeds, as required

Directions:

Preheat the oven to 400 degrees F. Line a baking sheet with parchment paper.

In a pan of water, arrange a steamer basket.

Place the sweet potato in steamer basket and steam approximately 10-15 minutes.

In a sizable bowl, put the sweet potato.

Add coconut milk and mash well.

Add remaining ingredients except flax seeds and mix till well combined.

Make about 1½-2-inch balls from your mixture.

Arrange the balls onto prepared baking sheet inside a single layer.

Sprinkle with flax seeds.

Bake for around 20-25 minutes.

Nutrition:

Calories: 464 Fat: 12g, Carbohydrates: 20g, Fiber: 8g, Protein: 27g

Coconut & Banana Cookies

Servings: 7

Preparation Time: 15 minutes

Cooking Preparation Time: 25 minutes

Ingredients:

2 cups unsweetened coconut, shredded

3 medium bananas, peeled

½ teaspoon ground cinnamon

½ teaspoon ground turmeric

Pinch of salt and freshly ground black pepper

Directions:

Preheat the oven to 350 degrees F. Line a cookie sheet having a lightly greased parchment paper.

In a mixer, add all ingredients and pulse till a dough like mixture forms.

Make small balls through the mixture and set onto prepared cookie sheet in a single layer.

With your fingers, gently press along the balls in order to create the cookies.

Bake for about 15-20 min or till golden brown.

Nutrition:

Calories: 370 Fat: 4g, Carbohydrates: 28g, Fiber: 11g, Protein: 33g

Fennel Seeds Cookies

Servings: 5

Preparation Time: 10 minutes

Cooking Preparation Time: 20 minutes

Ingredients:

1/3 cup coconut flour

¼ teaspoon whole fennel seeds

½ teaspoon fresh ginger, grated finely

¼ cup coconut oil, softened

2 tablespoons raw honey

1 teaspoon vanilla extract

Pinch of ground cinnamon

Pinch of salt and freshly ground black pepper

Directions:

Preheat the oven to 360 degrees F. Line a cookie sheet which has a parchment paper.

In a substantial bowl, add all ingredients and mix till an even dough form.

Make small balls in the mixture make onto prepared cookie sheet inside a single layer.

With your fingers, gently press along the balls in order to create the cookies.

Bake approximately 9 minutes or till golden brown.

Nutrition:

Calories: 353 Fat: 5g, Carbohydrates: 19g, Fiber: 3g, Protein: 25g

Almond Scones

Servings: 6

Preparation Time: 10 minutes

Cooking Preparation Time: 20 minutes

Ingredients:

1 cup almonds

1 1/3 cups almond flour

¼ cup arrowroot flour

1 tablespoon coconut flour

1 teaspoon ground turmeric

Salt and freshly ground black pepper, to taste

1 egg

¼ cup essential olive oil

3 tablespoons raw honey

1 teaspoon vanilla flavoring

Directions:

In a mixer, add almonds and pulse till chopped roughly

Transfer the chopped almonds in a big bowl.

Add flours and spices and mix well.

In another bowl, add remaining ingredients and beat till well combined.

Add flour mixture into egg mixture and mix till well combined.

Arrange a plastic wrap over cutting board.

Place the dough over cutting board.

With both your hands, pat into about 1-inch thick circle.

Carefully, cut the circle in 6 wedges.

Arrange the scones onto a cookie sheet in a single layer.

Bake for approximately 15-twenty minutes.

Nutrition:

Calories: 304 Fat: 3g, Carbohydrates: 22g, Fiber: 6g, Protein: 20g

Chapter 8. Snacks & Appetizers

Parsnip Fries

Servings: 4

Preparation Time: 15 minutes

Cooking Preparation Time: 40 minutes

Ingredients:

2 tablespoons extra-virgin organic olive oil

1¼ pound small parsnips, peeled and quartered

1½ tablespoons fresh ginger, minced

Salt and freshly ground black pepper, to taste

Directions:

Preheat the oven to 325 degrees F.

In a 13x9-inch baking dish, place the oil evenly.

Add remaining ingredients and toss to coat well.

With a foil paper, cover the baking dish and bake for about 40 minutes.

Serve immediately.

Nutrition:

Calories: 178, Fat: 13g, Carbohydrates: 15g, Fiber: 1g, Protein: 11g

Sweet Potato Fries

Servings: 2

Preparation Time: 10 minutes

Cooking Preparation Time: 25 minutes

Ingredients:

1 large sweet potato, peeled and cut into wedges

1 teaspoon ground turmeric

1 teaspoon ground cinnamon

Salt and freshly ground black pepper, to taste

2 tablespoons extra-virgin olive oil

Directions:

Preheat the oven to 425 degrees F. Line a baking sheet having a foil paper.

In a sizable bowl, add all ingredients and toss to coat well.

Transfer the mixture into prepared baking sheet.

Bake for around 25 minutes, flipping once after 15 minutes.

Serve immediately.

Nutrition:

Calories: 211, Fat: 14g, Carbohydrates: 23g, Fiber: 6g, Protein: 4g

Okra Fries

Servings: 4

Preparation Time: 15 minutes

Cooking Preparation Time: 35 minutes

Ingredients:

2 tablespoons olive oil, divided

3 tablespoons creole seasoning

½ teaspoon ground turmeric

1 teaspoon water

1-pound okra, trimmed and slit in middle

Directions:

Preheat the oven to 450 degrees F. Line a baking sheet which has a foil paper and grease with 1 tablespoon of oil.

In a bowl, mix together creole seasoning, turmeric and water.

Fill the slits of okra with turmeric mixture.

Place the okra onto prepared baking sheet in a very single layer.

Bake for around 30-35 minutes, flipping once inside middle way.

Nutrition:

Calories: 198, Fat: 10g, Carbohydrates: 25g, Fiber: 5g, Protein: 15g

Potato Sticks

Servings: 2

Preparation Time: 15 minutes

Cooking Preparation Time: 10 min

Ingredients:

1 large russet potato, peeled and cut into 1/8-inch thick sticks lengthwise

10 curry leaves

¼ teaspoon ground turmeric

¼ teaspoon red chili powder

Salt, to taste

1 tbsp. essential olive oil

Directions:

Preheat the oven to 400 degrees F. Line 2 baking sheets with parchment papers.

In a sizable bowl, add all ingredients and toss to coat well.

Transfer the amalgamation into prepared baking sheets in the single layer.

Bake for around 10 minutes.

Serve immediately.

Nutrition:

Calories: 187 Fat: 9g, Carbohydrates: 26g, Fiber: 1g, Protein: 14g

Zucchini Chips

Servings: 2

Preparation Time: 15 minutes

Cooking Preparation Time: 15 minutes

Ingredients:

1 medium zucchini, cut into thin slices

1/8 teaspoon ground turmeric

1/8 teaspoon ground cumin

Salt, to taste

2 teaspoons essential olive oil

Directions:

Preheat the oven to 400 degrees F. Line 2 baking sheets with parchment papers.

In a substantial bowl, add all ingredients and toss to coat well.

Transfer a combination into prepared baking sheets in a single layer.

Bake approximately 10-fifteen minutes.

Serve immediately.

Nutrition:

Calories: 181 Fat: 10g, Carbohydrates: 17g, Fiber: 9g, Protein: 24g

Beet Chips

Servings: 2

Preparation Time: 15 minutes

Cooking Preparation Time: 20 minutes

Ingredients:

1 beetroot, trimmed, peeled and sliced thinly

1 teaspoon garlic, minced

1 tablespoon nutritional yeast

½ teaspoon red chili powder

2 teaspoons coconut oil, melted

Directions:

Preheat the oven to 375 degrees F. Line a baking sheet using a parchment paper.

In a large bowl, add all ingredients and toss to coat well.

Transfer the mixture into prepared baking sheet in a very single layer.

Bake approximately twenty minutes, flipping once inside the middle way.

Serve immediately.

Nutrition:

Calories: 80, Fat: 4.5g, Carbohydrates: 6g, Fiber: 2g, Protein: 3g

Beet Greens Chips

Servings: 2

Preparation Time: 15 minutes

Cooking Preparation Time: 25 minutes

Ingredients:

1 large bunch beet greens, tough ribs removed

Salt and freshly ground black pepper, to taste

Olive oil, as required

Directions:

Preheat the oven to 350 degrees F. Line a baking sheet having a parchment paper.

In a sizable bowl, add all ingredients and toss to coat well.

Transfer the leaves into prepared baking sheet inside a single layer.

Bake for approximately 25 minutes, flipping once after fifteen minutes.

Serve immediately.

Nutrition:

Calories: 204 Fat: 4g, Carbohydrates: 17g, Fiber: 6g, Protein: 7g

Spinach Chips

Servings: 1 serving

Preparation Time: 10 minutes

Cooking Preparation Time: 8 minutes

Ingredients:

2 cups fresh spinach leaves

Few drops of extra-virgin olive oil

Salt, to taste

Italian seasoning, to taste

Directions:

Preheat the oven to 325 degrees F. Line a baking sheet with a parchment paper.

In a substantial bowl, add spinach leaves and drizzle with oil.

With the hands, rub the spinach leaves till al the leaves are coated with oil.

Transfer the leaves into prepared baking sheet in a very single layer.

Bake for about 8 minutes.

Serve immediately.

Nutrition:

Calories: 200 Fat: 11g, Carbohydrates: 12g, Fiber: 8g, Protein: 16g

Plantain Chips

Servings: 1 serving

Preparation Time: 15 minutes

Cooking Preparation Time: 10 minutes

Ingredients:

1 plantain, peeled and sliced

½ teaspoon ground turmeric

Salt, to taste

1 teaspoon coconut oil, melted

Directions:

In a large bowl, add all ingredients and toss to coat well.

Transfer the half in the mixture in a large greased microwave safe bowl.

Microwave on high for around 3 minutes.

Now, decrease the capacity to 50% and microwave approximately 2 minutes.

Repeat with the remaining plantain mixture.

Nutrition:

Calories: 199 Fat: 9g, Carbohydrates: 14g, Fiber: 7g, Protein: 8g

Apple Chips

Servings: 8

Preparation Time: 15 minutes

Cooking Preparation Time: couple of hours

Ingredients:

Salt and freshly ground black pepper, to taste

2 tablespoons ground cinnamon

1 tablespoon ground ginger

1½ teaspoons ground cloves

1½ teaspoons ground nutmeg

3 Fuji apples, sliced thinly in rounds

Directions:

Preheat the oven to 200 degrees F. Line a baking sheet with a parchment paper.

In a bowl, mix together all spices.

Arrange the apple slices into prepared baking sheet in the single layer.

Sprinkle the apple slices with spice mixture generously.

Roast for around an hour.

Flip the medial side and sprinkle with spice mixture.

Serve immediately.

Bake approximately one hour.

Nutrition:

Calories: 177 Fat: 3g, Carbohydrates: 26g, Fiber: 9g, Protein: 8g

Sweet & Tangy Seeds Crackers

Servings: 10

Preparation Time: 15 minutes

Cooking Preparation Time: 12 hours

Ingredients:

2 cups water

1 cup sunflower seeds

1 cup flaxseeds

1 tablespoon fresh ginger, chopped

1 teaspoon raw honey

¼ cup freshly squeezed lemon juice

1 teaspoon ground turmeric

Salt, to taste

Directions

In a bowl, add water, sunflower seeds and flaxseeds and soak for around overnight.

Drain the seeds.

In a food processor, add soaked seeds and remaining ingredients and pulse till well combined.

Set dehydrator at 115 degrees F. Line a dehydrator tray with unbleached parchment paper.

Place the mix onto prepared dehydrator tray evenly.

With a knife, score how big crackers.

Dehydrate for about 12 hours.

Nutrition:

Calories: 193 Fat: 7g, Carbohydrates: 21g, Fiber: 7g, Protein: 26g

Fruit Crackers

Servings: 15

Preparation Time: 20 minutes

Cooking Preparation Time: 12 hours

Ingredients:

8 carrots

1 orange, peeled

1 apple

1 (1-inchpiece fresh ginger

1 onion

1 cup chia seeds

½ cup sesame seeds

1 tablespoon ground turmeric

Salt and freshly ground black pepper, to taste

Directions:

In a juicer, add carrots and extract juice based on manufacturer's directions.

In a bowl, transfer the carrot juice and pulp.

Now, in juicer, add orange, apple and ginger and extract the juice.

Transfer the juice inside the bowl with carrot juice and pulp.

In a food processor, add juice mixture and remaining ingredients and pulse till a puree forms.

Spread a combination into 3 dehydrator trays evenly.

With a knife, score how big crackers.

Set dehydrator at 115 degrees F.

Dehydrate for about 12 hours.

Nutrition:

Calories: 202, Fat: 5g, Carbohydrates: 20g, Fiber: 7g, Protein: 17g

Beet Crackers

Servings: 15

Preparation Time: 20 or so minutes

Cooking Preparation Time: 50 minutes

Ingredients:

1 cup raw beets, chopped

3 tablespoons arrowroot flour

3 tablespoons coconut flour

2 egg whites

1 tablespoon coconut oil

¼ teaspoon ground turmeric

1/8 teaspoon cayenne

Salt and freshly ground black pepper, to taste

Directions:

Preheat the oven to 350 degrees F. Grease a sizable baking sheet.

In a mixer, add beets and pulse till merely a puree forms.

Add remaining ingredients and pulse till well combined.

Place a parchment paper onto an easy surface.

Place the dough onto parchment paper and top with another paper.

With a rolling pin, roll the dough to at least one/8-inch thickness.

Remove the parchment papers.

Place the rolled dough onto prepared baking sheet.

Bake for around 40-50 minutes.

Nutrition:

Calories: 189 Fat: 7g, Carbohydrates: 23g, Fiber: 8g, Protein: 10g

Quinoa & Seeds Crackers

Servings: 6

Preparation Time: 15 minutes

Cooking Preparation Time: 20 or so minutes

Ingredients:

3 tablespoons water

1 tablespoon chia seeds

3 tablespoons sunflower seeds

1 tablespoon quinoa flour

1 teaspoon ground turmeric

Pinch of ground cinnamon

Salt, to taste

Directions:

Preheat the oven to 345 degrees F. Line a baking sheet with parchment paper.

In a bowl, add water and chia seeds and soak for approximately 15 minutes.

After fifteen minutes, add remaining ingredients and mix well.

Spread the mix onto prepared baking sheet.

Bake approximately 20 min.

Nutrition:

Calories: 200 Fat: 9g, Carbohydrates: 17g, Fiber: 5g, Protein: 10g

Apple Leather

Servings: 4

Preparation Time: 15 minutes

Cooking Preparation Time: 12 hours 25 minutes

Ingredients:

1 cup water

8 cups apples, peeled, cored and chopped

1 tablespoon ground cinnamon

2 tablespoons freshly squeezed lemon juice

Directions:

In a big pan, add water and apples on medium-low heat.

Simmer, stirring occasionally for around 10-15 minutes.

Remove from heat and make aside to cool slightly.

In a blender, add apple mixture and pulse till smooth.

Return the mixture into pan on medium-low heat.

Stir in cinnamon and fresh lemon juice and simmer approximately 10 minutes.

Transfer the mix onto dehydrator trays and with the back of spoon smooth the very best.

Set the dehydrator at 135 degrees F.

Dehydrate for around 10-12 hours.

Cut the apple leather into equal sized rectangles.

Now, roll each rectangle to make fruit rolls.

Nutrition:

Calories: 187 Fat: 7g, Carbohydrates: 15g, Fiber: 6g, Protein: 19g

Roasted Cashews

Servings: 16

Preparation Time: 5 minutes

Cooking Preparation Time: 20 or so minutes

Ingredients:

2 cups cashews

2 teaspoons raw honey

1½ teaspoons smoked paprika

½ teaspoon chili flakes

Salt, to taste

1 tablespoon freshly squeezed lemon juice

1 teaspoon organic olive oil

Directions:

Preheat the oven to 350 degrees F. Line a baking dish with a parchment paper.

In a bowl, add all ingredients and toss to coat well.

Transfer the cashew mixture into prepared baking dish inside a single layer.

Roast for approximately 20 min, flipping once inside middle way.

Remove from oven and make aside to cool completely before serving.

You can preserve these roasted cashews in airtight jar.

Nutrition:

Calories: 188 Fat: 7g, Carbohydrates: 12g, Fiber: 7g, Protein: 20g

Stuffed Mushrooms

Preparation Time: 30 minutes

Servings: 8

Ingredients:

1 lb. cremini mushrooms caps

3 tbsp. olive oil

A pinch of cayenne pepper

A pinch of smoked paprika

Onion dip

For the dip:

1 cup coconut cream

1/2 cup mayonnaise

2 tbsp. coconut oil

1 yellow onion; finely chopped

1/4 tsp. white pepper

1/4 tsp. garlic powder

2 tbsp. green onions chopped

Directions:

Heat up a pan with 2 tbsp. coconut oil over medium heat, add onion, garlic powder and white pepper, stir; cook for 10 minutes, take off heat and leave aside to cool down.

In a bowl; mix mayo with coconut cream, green onions and caramelized onions, stir well and keep in the fridge for now.

Season mushroom caps with a pinch of cayenne pepper and paprika and drizzle the olive oil over them.

Rub them, place on preheated grill over medium high heat and cook them for 5 minutes on each side. Arrange them on a platter, fill each with some of the onion dip and serve them cold!

Nutrition: Calories: 150; Fat: 3g; Fiber: 2g; Carbs: 4g; Protein: 6g

Avocado Boats

Preparation Time: 10 minutes

Servings: 2

Ingredients:

5 oz. canned tuna; drained and flaked

Juice of 1 lemon

1 avocado; pitted and cut in halves

Black pepper to the taste

1 tbsp. yellow onion; chopped

A pinch of sea salt

Directions:

Scoop most of the avocado flesh and put it in a bowl.

Add lemon juice, onion, black pepper to the taste, a pinch of salt and tuna and stir everything very well. Fill avocado cups with this mix and serve them.

Nutrition: Calories: 100; Fat: 2g; Fiber: 1g; Carbs: 3g; Protein: 5g

Pepperoni Bites

Preparation Time: 15 minutes

Servings: 24 pieces

Ingredients:

1/3 cup tomatoes; chopped

1/2 cup bell peppers; mixed and chopped

24 pepperoni sliced

1/2 cup paleo marinara sauce

4 oz. almond cheese; cubed

2 tbsp. basil; chopped

Black pepper to the taste

Directions:

Divide pepperoni slices into a muffin tray. Divide tomato and bell pepper pieces into pepperoni cups.

Also divide Paleo marinara sauce, basil and almond cheese cubes.

Sprinkle black pepper at the end, introduce cups in the oven at 400 °F and bake for 10 minutes.

Leave your pepperoni cups to cool down a bit, transfer them to a platter and serve.

Nutrition: Calories: 120; Fat: 2g; Fiber: 1g; Carbs: 3g; Protein: 5g

Egg Cups

Preparation Time: 25 minutes

Servings: 12

Ingredients:

A drizzle of avocado oil

12 eggs

8 asparagus spears; chopped

A pinch of sea salt

Black pepper to the taste

12 bacon strips; cooked

Directions:

Divide bacon strips into 12 muffin cups.

Crack an egg in each, add asparagus pieces on top, season with a pinch of sea salt and black pepper, place in the oven at 400 °F and bake for 15 minutes. Leave egg cups to cool down, transfer them to a platter and serve.

Nutrition: Calories: 200; Fat: 13g; Fiber: 1g; Carbs: 1g; Protein: 10g

Chapter 9. Lunch Recipes

Puttanesca-Style Greens and Beans

Servings: 6

Preparation Time: 15 minutes

Cooking Time: 1 hour

Ingredients

3 cups water

1 cup dried baby lima beans, soaked overnight

¾ cup pitted kalamata olives

½ cup pitted green olives

½ cup sundried tomatoes in olive oil (optional)

1 small yellow onion

2 cloves garlic

2 teaspoons capers

2 tablespoons extra-virgin olive oil

2 cups shredded greens (kale, chard, dandelion greens, or beet greens all work well)

4 anchovies, or 1–2 teaspoons anchovy paste (optional)

½ teaspoon black pepper

Directions

Combine the water and lima beans in a large saucepan and bring them to a boil over medium-high heat. After it boils, reduce the heat to low, cover, and simmer for about 45 minutes. You want the beans to be tender. When they are, drain well.

Combine the olives, sundried tomatoes, onion, garlic, and capers in a food processor and pulse until roughly chopped.

Heat 2 tablespoons of oil over medium-high heat in a large skillet. When hot, add the olive mixture and cook for about 5 minutes, or until the onions are soft.

Add the greens, anchovies, and black pepper. Stir and cook about 4 more minutes, and then stir in the beans. Heat through, and serve.

Nutrition:

Calories 314, fat 19 g, carbs 28 g, protein 8 g, sodium 927 mg

Mediterranean Quinoa Bowls

Servings: 6

Preparation Time: 15 minutes

Ingredients

Roasted Red Pepper Sauce:

1 (16 ounce) jar roasted red peppers, drained (or roast your own)

1 clove garlic

½ teaspoon salt (more to taste)

Juice of one lemon

¼ cup olive oil

½ cup almonds

For the bowls:

3 cups cooked quinoa

3 cups spinach or kale

1 cup chopped cucumber

½ cup feta cheese

½ cup kalamata olives

1 cup red onion, thinly sliced

Options:

hummus

fresh basil or parsley

olive oil, lemon juice, salt, pepper

Directions

Prepare the sauce. In a food processor, combine the sauce ingredients and pulse until mixture is just about smooth. It should be thick.

Build the bowls. Start with a serving of the cooked quinoa. Top with red pepper sauce, and then add a portion of the other toppings.

Nutrition:

Calories 407, fat 23 g, carbs 41 g, protein 11 g, sodium 853 mg

Leek and Chard Frittata

Servings: 5

Preparation Time: 5 minutes

Cooking Time: 35 minutes

Ingredients

1 tablespoon olive or avocado oil, more as needed

1 leek, finely chopped

1 ½ cup potatoes, diced

1 cup chard, chopped

1 teaspoon fine sea salt, divided

1 clove garlic, minced

½ cup cherry tomatoes

10 large eggs

½ teaspoon black pepper

½ teaspoon paprika

½ teaspoon turmeric

Directions

Preheat the oven to 375°F.

Heat the oil in an ovenproof skillet.

When it is hot, cook the leeks for 1–2 minutes, and then add the potatoes and cook 5 more minutes.

Add the chard to the skillet and cook until it is soft. Sprinkle with half of the salt and add the garlic and tomatoes.

Whisk together the eggs, remaining salt, pepper, paprika, and turmeric, and pour the mixture into the skillet.

Move the skillet to the oven and bake for about 25 minutes, or until set.

Nutrition:

Calories 224, fat 12 g, carbs 13 g, protein 14 g, sodium 684 mg

Greek Turkey Burgers with Tzatziki

Servings: 4

Preparation Time: 20 minutes

Cooking Time: 35 minutes

Ingredients

Turkey Burgers

1 tablespoon extra-virgin olive oil

½ cup sweet onion, minced

2 cloves garlic, minced

1 egg

½ cup chopped fresh parsley

½ teaspoon dried oregano

¼ teaspoon red pepper flakes

1 pound ground turkey

¾ cup bread crumbs

Salt and freshly ground black pepper to taste

1 batch tzatziki sauce, for serving

4 hamburger buns, for serving

Directions

Preheat the oven to 375°F.

In a small skillet over medium, heat the oil and sauté the onions and garlic until soft. Set aside until they are cool.

Once cooled, mix the aromatics together with the egg, parsley, oregano, red pepper flakes, and ground turkey. Stir in the breadcrumbs, season with salt and pepper, and mix gently until completely combined. Form the mixture into four patties.

Spray an ovenproof skillet with non-stick cooking spray, then heat it over medium-high heat. Place the patties in the skillet and sear them on both sides, about 2 minutes on each side.

Move the skillet to the oven and cook for about 15 minutes, or until the burgers are cooked through.

While waiting for the burgers to cook, prepare the tzatziki sauce by mixing together all the ingredients.

When burgers are done, top with tzatziki sauce and whatever other toppings you desire.

Nutrition:

Calories 326, fat 14 g, carbs 22 g, protein 27 g, sodium 109

Seared Ahi Tuna Poke Salad

Servings: 6

Preparation Time: 20 minutes | Cooking time105 minutes

Ingredients

Seared Ahi Tuna Poke

20 square wonton wrappers cut into strips (use corn tortillas to make this gluten free)

2 tablespoons olive oil

¼ cup soy sauce

1 teaspoon cornstarch

¼ cup pineapple juice

¼ cup honey

1 teaspoon chili garlic sauce or sriracha

2 tablespoons toasted sesame oil

6 (4 ounce) ahi tuna steaks

2 tablespoons black and white sesame seeds, toasted

For the salad

4–8 cups spring greens

½ cup fresh cilantro

1 cup fresh pineapple, diced

1 avocado, sliced

1 jalapeño or red chili, sliced

Hula Ginger Vinaigrette

(makes 1 ½ cups)

½ cup hot chili sesame oil or toasted sesame oil

¼ cup soy sauce

2 tablespoons pineapple juice

2 tablespoons rice vinegar

1 teaspoon chili garlic sauce or sriracha or more to taste

1 tablespoon tahini

1 lime, zested and juiced

2 teaspoons fresh ginger, grated

1 clove garlic, minced

1 tablespoon black and white sesame seeds, toasted

Directions

Preheat the oven to 400°F.

Grease a baking sheet with the olive oil and lay the wonton strips on it in a single layer. Sprinkle them with salt. Bake the strips for about 5 minutes, or until they are golden brown and crispy. Set the finished strips to the side for now.

Pour the soy sauce into a small saucepan, then whisk in the cornstarch until incorporated. Stir in the pineapple juice, honey, and chili sauce.

Over medium-high heat, bring the mixture to a boil, then reduce the temperature and simmer for 3–5 minutes, or until the sauce begins to thicken. Set the thickened sauce aside.

Pour the sesame oil in a large skillet, and heat over high heat. Sear the tuna steaks for 1–2 minutes on each side. Brush the thickened soy sauce mixture over each side and cook another 1–2 minutes. Baste with sauce so each side is well covered. When the steaks are done, sprinkle each side with sesame seeds.

Prepare the salad. In a salad bowl, combine the greens, cilantro, pineapple, avocado, and jalapeño pepper. Toss to combine.

Make the vinaigrette by combining all the ingredients and whisking well.

Plate the greens, top with seared tuna and wonton crisps. Top with some of the vinaigrette, and serve.

Nutrition:(before adding vinaigrette)

Calories 447, fat 18 g, carbs 45 g, protein 32 g, sodium 856 mg

Nutrition (serving = 2 tablespoons) (vinaigrette only)

Calories 103, fat 10 g, carbs 3 g, protein 1 g, sodium 346 mg

One-Pan Eggs with Asparagus and Tomatoes

Servings: 4

Preparation Time: 10 minutes

Cooking Time: 20 minutes

Ingredients

2 pounds asparagus

1 pint cherry tomatoes

2 tablespoons olive oil

4 eggs

2 teaspoons chopped fresh thyme

Salt and pepper to taste

Directions

Preheat the oven to 400°F.

Prepare a baking sheet by spraying it with non-stick cooking spray or olive oil.

Arrange the asparagus in an even layer on the sheet, and top it with the cherry tomatoes.

Pour the olive oil over the vegetables, and season them with salt and pepper.

Roast the vegetables until the asparagus is tender and tomatoes have softened (about 10 minutes).

Next, crack the eggs over the cooked vegetables and season with salt and pepper, and thyme.

Return the baking tray to the oven and cook until the egg whites are set, but the yolks are still soft.

Remove from oven and serve.

Nutrition:

Calories 158, fat 11 g, carbs 13 g, protein 11 g

Anti-Inflammatory Buddha Bowl

Servings: 4

Preparation Time: 10 minutes

Cooking Time: 30 minutes

Ingredients

2 pounds cauliflower florets, stems removed

1 tablespoon plus one teaspoon extra-virgin olive oil, divided

1 teaspoon turmeric

Salt and pepper

10 ounces kale, chopped

1 clove garlic, minced

8 medium beets, cooked, peeled, and chopped

2 avocados, cubed

2 cups fresh blueberries

⅓ cup raw walnuts, chopped

Directions

Preheat the oven to 425°F.

Cover a baking tray with foil and spray the foil with either coconut or olive oil.

Toss the cut cauliflower with 1 tablespoon of the olive oil and turmeric. Arrange it on the prepared baking tray. Season with salt and pepper and transfer the tray to the oven. Bake for about 30 minutes.

When the cauliflower is almost done, heat 1 teaspoon of olive oil in a large skillet. Add the kale and cook until it starts to wilt, then add the garlic.

When the cauliflower and kale are done, assemble the bowls. Start with kale, then top with cauliflower, beets, avocado, blueberries, and walnuts.

Serve, and enjoy!

Nutrition:

Calories 450, fat 27 g, carbs 49 g, protein 13 g, sodium 377 mg

Honey Ginger Shrimp Bowls

Servings: 2

Preparation Time: 20 minutes

Cooking Time: 6 minutes

Ingredients

For the shrimp:

2 tablespoons honey

2 tablespoons coconut aminos or soy sauce

1 teaspoon fresh ginger, minced

2 cloves garlic, minced

12 ounces large uncooked shrimp, peeled and deveined

2 teaspoons avocado oil

Lime, sea salt, and freshly ground pepper to taste

For the salad:

4 cups greens of your choice

½ cup shredded carrots

½ cup shredded radishes

4 green onions, sliced

¼ cup cilantro, chopped

1 avocado, sliced

For the dressing:

2 tablespoons lime juice

2 tablespoons extra-virgin olive oil

2 teaspoons coconut aminos

1 tablespoon honey

1 clove garlic, minced

½ teaspoon ginger powder

Sea salt and pepper to taste

Directions

In a mixing bowl, whisk together the honey, coconut aminos (or soy sauce), ginger, and garlic as listed under shrimp ingredients.

Put the shrimp in a resealable bag and pour the marinade mixture in. Manipulate the bag to make sure all the shrimp are covered. Refrigerate while you are preparing the salad and dressing.

In a large skillet, heat the avocado oil over medium-high heat. When hot, add the shrimp and the marinade and cook for about 3 minutes. Turn the shrimp and cook for another 3 minutes or until the shrimp is fully cooked and sauce has thickened a bit. Season with lime juice, salt, and pepper.

Prepare the salad in a large bowl by mixing together all the ingredients.

Divide the salad into 2 servings, and top each with half the shrimp.

Prepare the dressing by whisking together all the ingredients.

Top the salad with dressing, and serve.

Nutrition:

Calories 516, fat 32 g, carbs 47 g, protein 12 g, sodium 636 mg

Salmon Cakes

Servings: 5

Preparation Time: 30 minutes

Cooking Time: 50 minutes

Ingredients

½ pound fresh salmon

1 tablespoon olive oil

Kosher salt and freshly ground black pepper

¼ cup olive oil

¼ cup unsalted butter

1 red onion, diced small

3 stalks celery, diced small

1 small red bell pepper, diced small

1 small yellow bell pepper, diced small

¼ cup minced fresh flat-leaf parsley

1 tablespoon capers, drained

½ teaspoon hot sauce

½ teaspoon Worcestershire sauce

1 teaspoon Old Bay seasoning

3 slices stale bread, crusts removed

½ cup mayonnaise

1 teaspoon mustard

2 eggs, lightly beaten

Directions

Preheat the oven to 375°F.

Cover a baking tray with parchment paper and place the salmon skin side down on the paper. Brush it with olive oil and bake for 15–20 minutes, or until it is just done.

Cool for 10 minutes, then put it in the fridge until it has cooled completely.

In a large skillet over medium-high, heat half the olive oil and half the butter. Add the onion, celery, peppers, parsley, capers, hot sauce, Worcestershire, Old Bay, and salt and pepper to taste. Let it cook about 15 minutes, or until the vegetables are soft. Remove it from the heat and let it cool.

Lightly toast the bread and crumble it up.

Using a fork, gently shred the cold salmon in a mixing bowl. Add the mayonnaise, mustard, and eggs. Then mix in the bread crumbs and the cooled vegetables.

Refrigerate the mixture for about 20 minutes, then shape it into patties. (It should make about 10 patties.)

In a large skillet, heat the remaining oil and butter. When it is hot, add the patties and cook for approximately 3–4 minutes on each side, until they are a nice golden brown. Transfer cooked patties to a paper towel lined plate to drain.

Nutrition:

Calories 503, fat 43 g, carbs 12 g, protein 17 g, sodium 458 mg

Tuna Salad with White Beans

Servings: 2

Preparation Time: 5 minutes

Ingredients

1 can white tuna, packed in olive oil

1 (15 ounce) can white kidney or cannellini beans, rinsed and drained

½ cup red or sweet onion, minced

¼ cup fresh parsley, minced

¼ cup celery, minced

1 tablespoon fresh basil, minced

1 tablespoon extra-virgin olive oil

2 teaspoons apple cider vinegar

Salt and pepper to taste

Directions

In a mixing bowl, break up the tuna in its oil. Add the beans.

Stir in the onion, parsley, basil, and celery. Mix everything together, ensuring that the tuna is well distributed.

Add the olive oil, vinegar, and salt and pepper. Stir again to combine.

Nutrition:

Calories 276, fat 11 g, carbs 23 g, protein 26 g, sodium 526 mg

Chapter 10.   Dinner Recipes

Sesame Ginger Salmon

Servings: 4

Preparation Time: 10 minutes

Cooking Time: 20 minutes

Ingredients

1 teaspoon sesame oil

2 tablespoons soy sauce

2 tablespoons fresh ginger, grated

2 cloves garlic, minced

2 tablespoons honey

½ teaspoon red pepper flakes

2 large zucchinis, halved lengthwise and thinly sliced

1 red onion, halved and thinly sliced

1 lime, quartered

4 (6 ounce) skinless salmon fillets

4 teaspoons sesame seeds

Directions

Preheat the oven to 350°F.

Cut four pieces of parchment paper that are large enough to wrap the salmon fillets.

In a mixing bowl, stir together the sesame oil, soy sauce, ginger, garlic, honey, and red pepper flakes.

Lay out your parchment paper. On it, arrange a quarter of the zucchini slices and a quarter of the red onion. Squeeze a quarter of the lime over the top.

Lay a salmon fillet on the vegetables and brush it with the sesame oil mixture. Top with sesame seeds.

Fold up the sides of the parchment paper, making sure the salmon is completely contained within.

Place the salmon packets on a baking tray and bake for 16–18 minutes, or until the salmon is cooked through.

Serve in parchment paper.

Nutrition:

Calories 468, fat 26 g, carbs 21 g, protein 39 g, sodium 184 mg

Sweet Turmeric Chicken with Asparagus

Servings: 4

Preparation Time: 5 minutes

Cooking Time: 25 minutes

Ingredients

2 tablespoons olive oil

⅓ cup coconut flour

1 teaspoon ground turmeric

4 skinless chicken thighs or breasts

2 cloves garlic, minced

Pinch red pepper flakes

1 pound asparagus, trimmed

¼ cup honey

Salt and pepper to taste

Directions

Preheat the oven to 375°F.

In an ovenproof skillet, heat the olive oil over medium-high heat.

In a mixing bowl, stir together the flour and turmeric and dredge the chicken in the mixture, making sure to cover both sides adequately.

Gently place the chicken in the hot oil and fry on both sides for about 3 minutes, or until chicken has browned.

When the chicken is brown, add the garlic, red pepper flakes, and asparagus, and drizzle everything with honey. Season with salt and pepper. Transfer the skillet to the oven and bake for 20 minutes, flipping the chicken and asparagus halfway through.

When the chicken has finished and the juices run clear, remove the skillet from the oven and serve.

Nutrition:

Calories 302, fat 11 g, carbs 30 g, protein 24 g, sodium 64 mg

Chicken and Cabbage Skillet

Servings: 4

Preparation Time: 5 minutes

Cooking Time: 20 minutes

Ingredients

1 ½ pounds chicken breast or thighs, cubed

1 tablespoon avocado oil

½ head cabbage, chopped

1 tablespoon turmeric

1 teaspoon garlic powder

½ teaspoon sea salt

3 carrots, peeled and grated

6 green onions, chopped

3 cups spinach or kale

2 cups brown rice, cooked, for serving

½ cup fresh cilantro, chopped

Directions

Heat the oil in a skillet over medium-high heat. When the oil is hot, add the chicken pieces and cook until browned on all sides.

Add the cabbage and cook until the cabbage is soft, then stir in the turmeric, garlic powder, and salt.

Add the carrots, green onions, and spinach, stirring once again.

Cook for about 3 more minutes, and remove the skillet from the heat.

Serve over brown rice, with cilantro on top.

Nutrition:

Calories 422, fat 10 g, carbs 39 g, protein 45 g, sodium 460 mg

Salmon with Zoodles and Avocado Pesto

Servings: 2

Preparation Time: 10 minutes

Cooking Time: 20 minutes

Ingredients

2 (6 ounce) salmon steaks

Salt and pepper to taste

2 cloves garlic, minced

1 teaspoon lemon zest

1 medium zucchini

1 avocado

1 tablespoon pesto

Juice of half a lemon

1 teaspoon black pepper

2 tablespoons Parmesan

Directions

Preheat the oven to 350°F and cover a baking tray with parchment paper.

Place the salmon on the tray and season it with salt and pepper.

In a small mixing bowl, combine the minced garlic with the lemon zest. Rub it onto the surface of the fish.

Transfer the tray to the oven, and bake until the salmon flakes easily with a fork (about 20 minutes).

Meanwhile, using a mandolin slicer, a spiralizer, or a sharp knife, cut up the zucchini.

In a small mixing bowl, mash together the avocado, pesto, lemon juice, and pepper. You can use more pepper if desired.

Blanch and plate the zoodles, and top them with the avocado mixture.

When the salmon is done, lay a piece of salmon on top of the zoodles and avocado. Sprinkle with Parmesan.

Nutrition:

Calories 502, fat 26 g, carbs 19 g, protein 48 g, sodium 244 mg

Curried Shrimp and Vegetables

Servings: 4

Preparation Time: 10 minutes

Cooking Time: 15 minutes

Ingredients

3 tablespoons coconut oil

1 onion, sliced

2 cups cauliflower, cut into florets

1 cup coconut milk

1 tablespoon curry powder

¼ cup fresh parsley, chopped

1 pound shrimp, tails removed

Directions

In a large skillet, melt the coconut oil over medium-high heat. Add the onion and cauliflower and cook until they are softened.

Add coconut milk, curry, and parsley to the skillet. (Feel free to add any other spices you like. Turmeric will give you an even bigger anti-inflammatory boost.) Cook for 2–3 more minutes.

Stir the shrimp into the skillet and cook until shrimp is opaque.

Nutrition:

Calories 332, fat 22 g, carbs 11 g, protein 24 g, sodium 309 mg

Chicken and Snap Pea Stir Fry

Servings: 4

Preparation Time: 10 minutes

Cooking Time: 10 minutes

Ingredients

2 tablespoons coconut oil

1 pound boneless skinless chicken breast, thinly sliced

1 bunch scallions, thinly sliced

2 cloves garlic, minced

1 red bell pepper, thinly sliced

2 cups snap peas

¼ cup soy sauce

2 tablespoons rice vinegar

1 teaspoon Sriracha

2 tablespoons sesame seeds, plus more for garnish

¼ cup chopped fresh cilantro, plus more for garnish

Optional: Brown rice or pasta, for serving

Directions

Heat the oil over medium-high heat in a large skillet. When it is hot, add the chicken and cook until it begins to brown. Remove it to a plate and keep it warm.

Add the scallions and garlic to the hot skillet, and cook for 1 minute.

Add the red pepper and peas and cook just until they are tender but crisp.

Stir in the chicken slices, soy sauce, vinegar, sriracha, and sesame seeds and cook 2 more minutes.

Remove from heat and mix in the cilantro.

Serve over rice or pasta if desired, garnished with sesame seeds and cilantro.

Nutrition:

Calories 275, fat 12 g, carbs 12 g, protein 29 g, sodium 1106 mg

Confetti Chicken with Brussel Sprouts

Servings: 4

Preparation Time: 5 minutes

Cooking Time: 15 minutes

Ingredients

3 tablespoons olive oil, divided

15–20 fresh Brussels sprouts, trimmed and halved lengthwise

1 ½ pounds boneless skinless chicken breast, cubed

1 small red onion, peeled and diced small

1 teaspoon salt

¼ teaspoon red pepper flakes

¼ cup balsamic vinegar

2 tablespoons honey

½ cup chicken broth

½ cup dried cranberries

½ cup roasted pumpkin seeds

Directions

Heat 2 tablespoons of olive oil in a large skillet and add the Brussel sprouts with the cut side down. Cook about 5 minutes, or until the sprouts have turned a golden brown.

Move the Brussel sprouts to the side of the skillet and turn the cut sides up.

Add the rest of the olive oil and the chicken pieces, together with the red onion. Cook for 5 minutes or until the chicken is almost done, stirring often.

Season with the salt and red pepper flakes, and add the vinegar, honey, and chicken broth, stirring to combine.

Turn down the heat and allow to cook for 5 minutes, uncovered, or until the chicken is cooked through.

Add the cranberries and pumpkin seeds. Stir to mix everything together, and serve.

Nutrition:

Calories 468, fat 17 g, carbs 37 g, protein 43 g, sodium 325 mg

Smoked Trout Lettuce Wraps

Servings: 4

Preparation Time: 15 minutes | Marinating time 30 minutes

Ingredients

2 medium carrots, peeled and cut into thin ribbons

½ unpeeled English cucumber, cut into thin ribbons

¼ cup shallots, thinly sliced

¼ cup jalapeño peppers with seeds, thinly sliced

2 tablespoons fresh lime juice or unseasoned rice vinegar

1 tablespoon sugar

1 tablespoon fish sauce

8 ounces skinless smoked trout fillets, cut into bite-sized pieces

1 cup grape tomatoes, halved

½ cup fresh mint leaves

½ cup fresh basil leaves, chopped

16 inner leaves of romaine lettuce (from about 2 hearts of romaine)

½ cup sweet chili sauce

¼ cup dry-roasted peanuts, chopped

Directions

In a large bowl, combine carrots and cucumber ribbons, shallots, jalapeños, lime juice, sugar, and fish sauce. Cover and marinate for 30 minutes.

After 30 minutes, add the trout pieces, tomatoes, mint, and basil to the mixture and stir to combine.

Using a slotted spoon to drain off the liquid as you go, fill the lettuce leaves and place them on a serving dish.

Pour some chili sauce over each filled leaf. Sprinkle with peanuts, and serve.

Nutrition:

Calories 423, fat 12 g, carbs 60 g, protein 33 g, sodium 1245 mg

Instant Pot Beef Stew and Sweet Potatoes

Servings: 6

Preparation Time: 10 minutes

Cooking Time: 15 minutes

Ingredients

1 tablespoon avocado oil

1 onion, diced

1 tablespoon ginger, minced

3 cloves garlic, minced

1 cup carrots, cut into large chunks

4 cups sweet potatoes, peeled and cubed

2 teaspoons dried oregano

2 teaspoons dried thyme

1 teaspoon sea salt

1 teaspoon freshly ground black pepper

1 cup pumpkin purée (no salt added)

2 cups beef bone broth

1 ½ pounds beef chuck (grass fed preferred)

½ cup fresh parsley, chopped

6 green onions, sliced

1 avocado, diced

Directions

Select the sauté option on your Instant Pot and pour in the avocado oil. Once it is hot, add the onion, ginger, carrots, sweet potato, oregano, thyme, salt, and pepper. Cook and stir about 3 minutes.

Press cancel on the Instant Pot and stir in the pumpkin and bone broth. Mix everything together. Crumble the ground beef on the top.

Set the Instant Pot to high pressure and cook for 5 minutes. After the 5 minutes, quick release the pressure.

Sprinkle with parsley and green onion, and serve with avocado on top.

Nutrition:

Calories 370, fat 14 g, carbs 33 g, protein 27 g, sodium 743 mg

Chicken Enchilada Cauliflower Rice Bowl

Servings: 4

Preparation Time: 20 minutes

Cooking Time: 3–6 hours

Ingredients

Red Chili Enchilada Chicken

4 boneless skinless chicken breasts

2 teaspoons chili powder

1 (8 ounce) bottle red enchilada sauce

Cilantro Lime Cauliflower Rice

1 medium head of cauliflower, chopped into florets (about 4 cups),

2 tablespoons olive oil

1 ½ teaspoons kosher salt

1 teaspoon chili powder

1 teaspoon ground cumin

2 cloves garlic, minced

2 tablespoons lime juice

2 tablespoons cilantro, chopped

Toppings:

1 cup black beans

1 cup tomatoes, chopped

½ cup black olives

1 cup cooked broccoli (roasted is good)

2 avocados, diced

½ cup cilantro

Directions

First, prepare the chicken by combining the chicken, chili powder, and enchilada sauce in a slow cooker. Cover and cook on LOW for 6 hours or HIGH for 3 hours. When the chicken is cooked, shred it and mix it thoroughly in the sauce.

Next, make the cauliflower rice. Process the cauliflower in a food processor until it becomes the size of white rice.

Heat the olive oil in a large skillet over medium-high heat. When it is hot, add the cauliflower, salt, chili powder, cumin, and minced garlic. Cook for about 5 minutes, stirring from time to time to make sure the "rice" doesn't stick.

After 5 minutes, add the lime juice and the chopped cilantro.

Fill the serving bowls with cauliflower and top with chicken, black beans, tomatoes, olives, cooked broccoli, avocado, and extra cilantro.

Nutrition:

Calories 608, fat 31 g, carbs 38 g, protein 50 g, sodium 1366 mg

Slow Cooker Jambalaya

Servings: 12

Preparation Time: 20 minutes

Cooking Time: 7–8 hours

Ingredients

1 pound boneless skinless, chicken breasts, cut into 1-inch cubes

1 pound andouille sausage, sliced

1 pound black forest ham, cubed

1 cup celery, diced

1 sweet potato, diced

1 cup cauliflower florets

1 cup onion, chopped

1 large green bell pepper, chopped

1 cup okra, chopped

1 cup chicken broth

1 teaspoon dried thyme

1 teaspoon dried parsley

1 teaspoon dried oregano

1 tablespoon Cajun seasoning

1 teaspoon chili powder

1 (28-ounce) can diced tomatoes with juice

1 teaspoon cayenne pepper

Directions

Plug in your slow cooker add all the ingredients.

Cook on LOW for 7–8 hours.

Nutrition:

Calories 245, fat 13 g, carbs 9 g, protein 22 g, sodium 998 mg

Arugula & Quinoa Tabbouleh

Servings: 6

Preparation Time: 10 Minutes

Calories: 235

Protein: 5 Grams

Fat: 14 Grams

Carbs: 24 Grams

Ingredients:

½ Cup Flat Leaf Parsley, Fresh & Chopped

3 Cups Quinoa, Cooked

1 Cup Arugulas, Packed

4 Scallions, Sliced

½ Cup Tomato, Diced

½ Cup Mint Leaves, Fresh & Minced

1/3 Cup Olive Oil

½ Teaspoon Garlic Powder

½ Teaspoon Sea Salt, Fine

Black Pepper to Taste

2 Tablespoons Lemon Juice, Fresh

Directions:

Mix together your tomato, parsley, mint, scallions, arugula and quinoa.

In a bowl whisk together your lemon juice, garlic, salt, pepper and olive oil.

Toss your salad in the dressing before serving.

Wild Rice Salad

Servings: 8

Preparation Time: 25 Minutes

Calories: 143

Protein: 5 Grams

Fat: 4 Grams

Carbs: 22 Grams

Ingredients:

3 Cups Wild Rice, Cooked

2 Tablespoons Ghee

3 Cloves Garlic, Minced

1 Sweet Onion, Small & Diced

2 Cups Cremini Mushrooms, Sliced

½ Teaspoon Thyme, Dried

½ Cup Vegetable Broth

½ Teaspoon Sea Salt, Fine

Directions:

Place your rice in a bowl before setting it to the side.

Get out a saucepan, placing it over medium heat. Melt your ghee before adding in your garlic and onion. Cook for five minutes, and make sure to stir frequently.

Stir in your broth, thyme, salt and mushrooms. Allow it to cook for even to ten minutes. Your mushrooms should be tender, and the broth should reduce by half.

Add in the rice and mushroom mixture. Stir well, and serve warm.

Sweet Korean Lentils

Servings: 4

Preparation Time: 30 Minutes

Calories: 281

Protein: 14 Grams

Fat: 5 Grams

Carbs: 45 Grams

Ingredients:

1 Tablespoon Avocado Oil

1 White Onion, Small & Diced

2 Cloves Garlic, Minced

2 Cups Vegetable Broth

1 Cup Lentils, Dried, Sorted & Rinsed

3 Tablespoons Coconut Aminos

1 Teaspoon Sesame Oil

1 Tablespoon Rice Vinegar

¼ Teaspoon Red Pepper Flakes

½ Teaspoon Ginger, Ground

1 Tablespoon Sesame Seeds

2 Scallions, Sliced

Directions:

Get out a stockpot, placing it over medium heat before adding in your avocado oil, garlic and onion. Sauté, cooking for five minutes. The onion should be translucent.

Add in your lentils, coconut aminos, broth, vinegar, sesame oil, ginger, coconut sugar, ginger, and red pepper flakes.

Increase your heat to medium-high, bringing it to a simmer. Reduce your heat to low, and then cover. Allow it to cook for fifteen minutes. The lentils should be cooked. Garnish with scallions and sesame seeds.

Citrus Spinach

Servings: 4

Preparation Time: 20 Minutes

Calories: 80

Protein: 1 Gram

Fat: 7 Grams

Carbs: 4 Grams

Ingredients:

2 Tablespoons Olive Oil

2 Cloves Garlic, Minced

4 Cups Baby Spinach, Fresh

½ Orange, Juiced & Zested

½ Teaspoon Sea Salt

1/8 Teaspoon Black Pepper

Directions:

Get out a large skillet, placing it over medium-high heat. Heat you olive oil until it begins to shimmer.

Add in your spinach, and cook for three minutes. Make sure to stir occasionally.

Add in your garlic, cooking for another thirty seconds. You'll need to stir constantly.

Add in your orange zest, orange juice, salt and pepper, cooking for two more minutes. Stir constantly until your juice evaporates, and then serve warm.

Brown Rice & Bell Pepper

Servings: 4

Preparation Time: 20 Minutes

Calories: 266

Protein: 5 Grams

Fat: 8 Grams

Carbs: 44 Grams

Ingredients:

2 Cups Brown Rice, Cooked

2 Tablespoon Soy Sauce, Low Sodium

2 Tablespoons Olive Oil

1 Red Bell Pepper, Chopped

1 Green Bell Pepper, Chopped

1 Onion, Chopped

Directions:

Get out a nonstick skillet, placing it over medium-high heat. Add in your olive oil, heating it up until it shimmers.

Add in your onion and bell pepper, cooking for seven minutes. Make sure to stir frequently. The vegetable should brown.

Add in your soy sauce and rice, cooking or three minutes. Stir constantly. Your rice should be warmed.

Green Pasta Salad

Servings: 4

Preparation Time: 30 Minutes

Calories: 450

Protein: 13 Grams

Fat: 15 Grams

Carbs: 68 Grams

Ingredients:

2 Cups Arugula

1 Cup Basil Sauce

1 Tablespoon Olive Oil

1 Bunch Asparagus, Sliced into 1 Inch Pieces

12 Ounces Penne

2 Scallions, Sliced

Sea Salt & Black Pepper to Taste

Directions:

Start by cooking your pasta per package instructions, and add in your asparagus for the last two minutes.

Drain this mixture using a colander before putting them back in the pot.

Add in your sauce and oil, stirring until it's combined.

Allow it to cool to room temperature, and then stir in your remaining ingredients. Serve warm.

163

Roasted Potatoes

Servings: 4

Preparation Time: 25 Minutes

Calories: 180

Protein: 3 Grams

Fat: 7 Grams

Carbs: 27 Grams

Ingredients:

2 Tablespoons Olive Oil

1 ½ lbs. Fingerling Potatoes, Scrubbed

1 Teaspoon Sea Salt, Fine

¼ Teaspoon Black Pepper

1 Tablespoon Parsley, Fresh & Chopped

Directions:

Start by heating your oven to 400, and then get out a baking sheet. Brush it with oil, and place your potatoes in a bowl. Toss with two tablespoons of oil. It should be coated. Season with salt and pepper, and arrange on a baking sheet in a single layer.

Bake for twenty minutes. They should be tender and browned lightly. Sprinkle with parsley before serving.

Rosemary Rice

Servings: 4

Preparation Time: 55 Minutes

Calories: 190

Protein: 6 Grams

Fat: 4 Grams

Carbs: 33 Grams

Ingredients:

1 Cup Wild Rice

3 ½ Cups Vegetable Broth

1 Teaspoon Sea Salt, Fine

1 Tablespoon Olive Oil

¼ Teaspoon Black Pepper

1 Teaspoon Rosemary, Fresh & Chopped

Directions:

Rinse your rice using a fine mesh strainer, and drain well. Place it in a pot, adding in your broth, salt, pepper and olive oil.

Bring it to a boil using high heat before reducing it to simmer. Cover the pot partially so that steam escapes. Allow it to cook for thirty-five to forty-five minutes.

Drain any remaining liquid, adding your rosemary, and fluff before serving.

Broccoli Slaw

Servings: 4

Preparation Time: 10 Minutes

Calories: 110

Protein: 2 Grams

Fat: 7 Grams

Carbs: 12 rams

Ingredients:

¼ Cup Cranberries, Dried

¼ Cup Almonds, Sliced

2 Scallions, Sliced

1 Head Broccoli, Chopped into Bite Size Pieces

1 Tablespoon Paleo Mayonnaise

2 Tablespoons Whole Milk Yogurt, Plain

1 Tablespoon Lemon Juice, Fresh

1 Teaspoon Honey, Raw

½ Teaspoon Ground Cumin

Dash Hot Sauce

Sea Salt & Black Pepper to Taste

Directions:

Combine your scallions, cranberries, almonds and broccoli together.

Get out a different bowl and whisk your remaining ingredients together to make your dressing. Pour this over your broccoli mixture, and mix well before serving.

Sautéed Bok Choy

Servings: 4

Preparation Time: 20 Minutes

Calories: 143

Protein: 12 Grams

Fat: 5 Grams

Carbs: 21 Grams

Ingredients:

2 Tablespoons Coconut Aminos

1 Tablespoon Sesame Oil

1 Teaspoon Ginger, Peeled & Minced

2 Cloves Garlic, Minced

3 Tablespoons Water

1 Teaspoon Rice Vinegar

¼ Teaspoon Red Pepper Flakes

4 Heads Bok Choy, Halved Lengthwise

Directions:

Get out a large saucepan, placing it over medium heat. Warm your sesame oil before adding in your garlic and ginger. Cook for two minutes.

Stir in your vinegar, coconut aminos, red pepper flakes and water before adding your bok choy. Make sure that the cut sides are placed down, and then lower the heat to low. Cover your pan, allowing them to steam for five to ten minutes. They should be tender. Serve warm.

Mixed Beet Salad

Servings: 6

Preparation Time: 5 Minutes

Calories: 107

Protein: 4 Grams

Fat: 4 Grams

Carbs: 15 Grams

Ingredients:

6 Cups Mixed Greens

1 Cup English Peas, Shelled, Frozen & Thawed

3 Small Chioggia Beets, Sliced Thin

1 Red Onion, Small & Sliced

1 Avocado, Sliced

¼ Cup Lemon Dijon Mustard Dressing

Directions:

Mix everything together and then toss with the dressing before serving.

Root Mash

Servings: 4

Preparation Time: 30 Minutes

Calories: 270

Protein: 2 Grams

Fat: 10 Grams

Carbs: 23 Grams

Ingredients:

2 Cups Sweet Potatoes, Chopped

2 Cups Celery Root, Chopped, Trimmed & Peeled

1 Teaspoon Lemon Juice, fresh

2 Tablespoons Ghee

½ Teaspoon Sea Salt, Fine

Pinch Cayenne Pepper

Directions:

Get a steamer basket, placing it over boiling water. Place your celery root and sweet potatoes in it, steaming for twenty-five minutes using medium heat. They should be tender.

Place them in a food processor, blending until smooth and then add in your remaining ingredients. Pulse until well combined, and serve warm.

Citrus Roasted Cauliflower

Servings: 4

Preparation Time: 25 Minutes

Calories: 138

Protein: 3 Grams

Fat: 11 Grams

Carbs: 9 Grams

Ingredients:

1 ½ Teaspoons Ground Cumin

1 Teaspoon Sea Salt, Fine

½ Teaspoon Chili Powder

½ Teaspoon Black Pepper

1 Head Cauliflower, Chopped Into Bite Size pieces

½ Teaspoon Garlic Powder

3 Tablespoons Ghee, Melted

3 Tablespoons Lime Juice, Fresh

Directions:

Start by heating your oven to 450.

Get out a bowl and mix your garlic, cumin, chili powder, salt and pepper.

Spread your cauliflower out evenly in a baking pan, drizzling with ghee and lime juice, sprinkling it with the spice mixture. Toss to make sure it's coated.

Bake for fifteen minutes.

Roasted Vegetables

Servings: 4

Preparation Time: 30 Minutes

Calories: 184

Protein: 2 Grams

Fat: 14 Grams

Carbs: 15 Grams

Ingredients:

2 Zucchini, Diced into 1 Inch Pieces

1 Red Bell Pepper, Diced into 1 Inch Pieces

1 Red Onion, Diced into 1 Inch Pieces

1 Yellow Bell Pepper, Diced into 1 Inch pieces

1 Sweet Potato, Diced into 1 Inch Pieces

4 Cloves Garlic

¼ Cup Olive Oil

1 Teaspoon Sea Salt, Fine

Directions:

Start by heating your oven to 450.

Line your baking sheet with foil, and then get out a bowl.

Toss your bell pepper, onion, zucchini, sweet potato, olive oil, salt and garlic. Spread this mixture out evenly on the baking sheet.

Bake for twenty-five minutes, stirring halfway through.

Chapter 11.   Dessert Recipes

Avocado Fudge

Servings: 16

Preparation Time: 3 Hours 15 Minutes

Calories: 120

Protein: 1 Gram

Fat: 9 Grams

Carbs: 11 Grams

Ingredients:

1 Avocado, Peeled & Pitted

½ Teaspoon Sea Salt

¼ Cup Coconut Oil

1 ½ Cup Chocolate Chips, Bittersweet

Directions:

Get out an eight-inch square baking pan, and then line it with parchment paper. Get out a double boiler, and melt your coconut oil and chocolate together.

Transfer it to a food processor, allowing it to cool a little before adding in your avocado. Process until it is smooth.

Spread this mixture into your pan, sprinkling with sea salt.

Place it in the fridge for three hours before cutting it into sixteen pieces.

Caramelized Pears

Servings: 4

Preparation Time: 25 Minutes

Calories: 290

Protein: 12 Grams

Fat: 11 Grams

Carbs: 41 Grams

Ingredients:

1 Teaspoon Cinnamon

2 Tablespoon Honey, Raw

1 Tablespoon Coconut Oil

4 Pears, Peeled, Cored & Quartered

2 Cups Yogurt, Plain

¼ Cup Toasted Pecans, Chopped

1/8 Teaspoon Sea Salt

Directions:

Get out a large skillet, and then heat the oil over medium-high heat.

Add in your honey, cinnamon, pears and salt. Cover, and allow it to cook for four to five minutes. Stir occasionally, and your fruit should be tender.

Uncover it, and allow the sauce to simmer until it thickens. This will take several minutes.

Soon your yogurt into four dessert bowls. Top with pears and pecans before serving.

Berry Ice Pops

Servings: 4

Preparation Time: 3 Hours 5 Minutes

Calories: 140

Protein: 5 Grams

Fat: 4 Grams

Carbs: 23 Grams

Ingredients:

1 Cup Strawberries, Fresh or Frozen

2 Cups Whole Milk Yogurt, Plain

1 Cup Blueberries, Fresh or Frozen

¼ Cup Water

1 Teaspoon Lemon Juice, Fresh

2 Tablespoons Honey, Raw

Directions:

Place all of your ingredients in a blender, and blend until smooth.

Pour into your molds, and freeze for at least three hours before serving.

Fruit Cobbler

Servings: 8

Preparation Time: 30 Minutes

Calories: 196

Protein: 4 Grams

Fat: 12 Grams

Carbs: 15 Grams

Ingredients:

1 Teaspoon Coconut Oil

¼ Cup Coconut Oil, Melted

2 Cups Peaches, Fresh & Sliced

2 Cups Nectarines, Fresh & Sliced

2 Tablespoons Lemon Juice, Fresh

¾ Cup Rolled Oats

¾ Cup Almond Flour

¼ Cup Coconut Sugar

½ Teaspoon Vanilla Extract, Pure

1 Teaspoon Ground Cinnamon

Dash Salt

Filter Water for Mixing

Directions:

Start by heating your oven to 425.

Get out a cast iron skillet, coating it with a teaspoon of coconut oil.

Mix your lemon juice, peaches and nectarines together in the skillet.

Get out a food processor, mixing your almond flour, oats, coconut sugar, and remaining coconut oil. Add in your cinnamon, vanilla and salt, pulsing until the oat mixture resembles a dry dough.

If you need more moisture, add filtered water a tablespoon at a time, and then break the dough into chunks, spreading it across the fruit.

Bake for twenty minutes before serving warm.

Chocolate Cookies

Servings: 12

Preparation Time: 20 Minutes

Calories: 226

Protein: 6 Grams

Fat: 15 Grams

Carbs: 20 Grams

Ingredients:

¾ Cup Almond Butter, Creamy

½ Cup Coconut Sugar

¼ Cup Cocoa Powder

1 Egg

1 Egg Yolk

2 Teaspoons Vanilla Extract, Pure

½ Cup Chocolate Chips, Semi Sweet

1 Teaspoon Baking Soda

¼ Teaspoon Salt

Dash Sea Salt

Directions:

Start by preheating your oven to 350, and then get out a baking sheet. Line it with parchment paper, and get out a bowl cream your almond butter, cocoa powder, vanilla and coconut sugar together.

Get out another bowl, whisking your egg and egg yolk together. Add this to your almond butter mixture. Stir to combine.

Stir in your baking soda, salt and chocolate chips.

Make twelve pieces, and roll them into balls. Place six per pan, and bake for nine to ten minutes.

Allow them to rest for five minutes before sprinkling with sea salt, and serve cooled.

Ginger Baked Apples

Preparation Time: 10 minutes

Cooking Preparation Time: 30 minutes

Servings: 4

Ingredients:

2 apples, cored and halved

1 tablespoon ginger, grated

1 tablespoon turmeric powder

¼ cup raw honey

1 tablespoon ginger, grated

Directions:

Arrange the apples in a baking dish, add the ginger and the other ingredients, and bake at 390 degrees F for 30 minutes.

Divide the apples mix between dessert plates and serve.

Nutrition: calories 90, fat 2, fiber 1, carbs 2, protein 5

Watermelon and Avocado Cream

Preparation Time: 2 hours

Cooking Preparation Time: 0 minutes

Servings: 4

Ingredients:

2 cups coconut cream

1 watermelon, peeled and chopped

2 avocados, peeled, pitted and chopped

1 tablespoon honey

2 teaspoons lemon juice

Directions:

In a blender, combine the watermelon with the cream and the other ingredients, pulse well, divide into bowls and keep in the fridge for 2 hours before serving.

Nutrition: calories 121, fat 2, fiber 2, carbs 6, protein 5

Strawberries Sorbet

Preparation Time: 2 hours

Cooking Preparation Time: 0 minutes

Servings: 6

Ingredients:

1 pound strawberries, halved and frozen

1 cup orange juice

1 tablespoon orange zest, grated

1 tablespoon honey

Directions:

In a blender, combine the strawberries with the orange zest and the other ingredients, pulse well, divide into bowls and keep in the freezer for 2 hours before serving.

Nutrition: calories 121, fat 1, fiber 2, carbs 2, protein 4

Lemony Pineapple Mix

Preparation Time: 10 minutes

Cooking Preparation Time: 0 minutes

Servings: 4

Ingredients:

2 tablespoons almonds, chopped

1 tablespoon walnuts, chopped

2 cups pineapple, peeled and roughly cubed

1 tablespoon lemon juice

Zest of 1 lemon, grated

½ teaspoon vanilla extract

A pinch of cinnamon powder

Directions:

In a bowl, combine the pineapple with the nuts and the other ingredients, toss and serve.

Nutrition: calories 215, fat 3, fiber 4, carbs 12, protein 8

Chia Pudding

Preparation Time: 30 minutes

Cooking Preparation Time: 0 minutes

Servings: 4

Ingredients:

2 cups almond milk

2 tablespoon honey

1 cup chia seeds

A pinch of cardamom powder

1 tablespoon lemon zest, grated

Directions:

In a bowl, mix the chia seeds with the almond milk and the other ingredients, toss, leave aside for 30 minutes, divide into small bowls and serve.

Nutrition: calories 199, fat 2, fiber 3, carbs 7, protein 5

Mango Smoothie

Preparation Time: 10 minutes

Cooking Preparation Time: 0 minutes

Servings: 2

Ingredients:

2 cups mango, peeled and c hopped

1 cup orange juice

1 tablespoon ginger, grated

1 teaspoon turmeric powder

Directions:

In your blender, combine the mango with the juice and the other ingredients, pulse well, divide into 2 glasses and serve cold.

Nutrition: calories 100, fat 1, fiber 2, carbs 4, protein 5

Coconut and Chocolate Cream

Preparation Time: 2 hours

Cooking Preparation Time: 0 minutes

Servings: 4

Ingredients:

2 cups coconut milk

2 tablespoons ginger, grated

2 tablespoons honey

1 cup dark chocolate, chopped and melted

½ teaspoon cinnamon powder

1 teaspoon vanilla extract

Directions:

In a blender, combine the coconut milk with the ginger and the other ingredients, pulse well, divide into bowls and keep in the fridge for 2 hours before serving.

Nutrition: calories 200, fat 3, fiber 5, carbs 12, protein 7

Cardamom Avocado Mix

Preparation Time: 10 minutes

Cooking Preparation Time: 0 minutes

Servings: 4

Ingredients:

2 avocados, peeled, pitted and cut into wedges

1 teaspoon cardamom, ground

½ cup coconut butter

1 cup coconut cream

1 teaspoon vanilla extract

Directions:

In your food processor, combine the avocados with the cream and the other ingredients, pulse well, divide into bowls and serve cold.

Nutrition: calories 211, fat 2, fiber 4, carbs 11, protein 7

Almond Strawberries Mix

Preparation Time: 10 minutes

Cooking Preparation Time: 20 minutes

Servings: 4

Ingredients:

1 pound strawberries, halved

2 tablespoons almonds, chopped

2 tablespoons coconut oil, melted

2 tablespoons lime juice

1 teaspoon vanilla extract

1 teaspoon honey

Directions:

Arrange the strawberries on a baking sheet lined with parchment paper, add the almonds and the other ingredients, toss and bake at 390 degrees F for 20 minutes.

Divide the strawberries mix into bowls and serve.

Nutrition: calories 220, fat 2, fiber 3, carbs 8, protein 2

Lime Apple Compote

Preparation Time: 10 minutes

Cooking Preparation Time: 20 minutes

Servings: 4

Ingredients:

Juice of 1 lime

1 pound apples, cored and cut into wedges

1 tablespoon honey

1 and ½ cups water

Directions:

In a pan, combine the apples with the lime juice and the other ingredients, toss, bring to a simmer and cook over medium heat fro 20 minutes.

Divide the mix into bowls and serve cold.

Nutrition: calories 108, fat 1, fiber 2, carbs 4, protein 7

Sweet Berries Mix

Preparation Time: 10 minutes

Cooking Preparation Time: 0 minutes

Servings: 4

Ingredients:

1 cup blackberries

1 cup blueberries

2 teaspoons lime zest, grated

1 tablespoon raw honey

½ teaspoon vanilla extract

1 cup almond milk

Directions:

In your blender, combine the berries with the lime zest and the other ingredients, pulse well, divide into bowls and serve.

Nutrition: calories 217, fat 7, fiber 8, carbs 10, protein 8

Maple Berries Mix

Preparation Time: 10 minutes

Cooking Preparation Time: 15 minutes

Servings: 4

Ingredients:

2 cups coconut milk

1 cup strawberries

¼ teaspoon vanilla extract

1/3 cup pure maple syrup

Directions:

In a small pot, combine the coconut milk with the berries and the other ingredients, toss, cook over medium heat for 15 minutes, divide into bowls and serve cold.

Nutrition: calories 176, fat 4, fiber 2, carbs 7, protein 6

Papaya and Apples Bowls

Preparation Time: 4 minutes

Cooking Preparation Time: 0 minutes

Servings: 4

Ingredients:

2 apples, cored and cut into wedges

1 cup papaya, roughly cubed

½ teaspoon vanilla extract

2 tablespoons almonds, chopped

1 tablespoon walnuts, chopped

2 tablespoons lemon juice

Directions:

In a bowl, combine the papaya with the apples and the other ingredients, toss, divide into smaller bowls and serve.

Nutrition: calories 140, fat 1, fiber 2, carbs 3, protein 5

Coconut Squares

Preparation Time: 2 hours

Cooking Preparation Time: 0 minutes

Servings: 4

Ingredients:

1/3 cup natural coconut butter, melted

1 and ½ tablespoons coconut oil

2 tablespoons orange juice

½ teaspoon orange zest, grated

1 tablespoons honey

Directions:

In a bowl, combine the coconut butter with the oil and the other ingredients, stir well, scoop into a square pan, spread well, cut into squares, keep in the freezer for 2 hours and serve.

Nutrition: calories 72, fat 4, fiber 2, carbs 8, protein 6

Chia and Mango mix

Preparation Time: 10 minutes

Cooking Preparation Time: 0 minutes

Servings: 4

Ingredients:

¼ cup chia seeds

1 cup almond milk

2 mangos, peeled and cubed

2 teaspoons vanilla extract

¼ cup coconut, shredded

1 tablespoon honey

Directions:

In a bowl, combine the chia seeds with the mango, the milk and the other ingredients, toss, leave aside for 10 minutes, divide into small bowls and serve.

Nutrition: calories 287, fat 17.2, fiber 5.1, carbs 34.6, protein 3.2

Pomegranate and Orange Mix

Preparation Time: 2 hours

Cooking Preparation Time: 0 minutes

Servings: 4

Ingredients:

½ cup coconut cream

1 orange, peeled and cut into wedges

1 teaspoon vanilla extract

½ cup almonds, chopped

1 cup pomegranate seeds

1 tablespoon orange zest, grated

Directions:

In a bowl, combine the orange with the pomegranate seeds and the other ingredients, toss and keep in the fridge for 2 hours before dividing into smaller bowls and serving.

Nutrition: calories 68, fat 5.1, fiber 4, carbs 6, protein 1

Almond and Berries Bowls

Preparation Time: 10 minutes

Cooking Preparation Time: 0 minutes

Servings: 4

Ingredients:

½ cup dates, pitted

½ teaspoon vanilla extract

1 cup almonds, chopped

1 cup blackberries

1 tablespoon maple syrup

1 tablespoon coconut oil, melted

Directions:

In a bowl, combine the berries with the almonds and the other ingredients, toss, divide into small cups and serve.

Nutrition: calories 130, fat 5, fiber 5, carbs 12, protein 4

Apple Cream

Preparation Time: 10 minutes

Cooking Preparation Time: 0 minutes

Servings: 4

Ingredients:

1 pounds apples, peeled, cored and cubed

2 cups coconut cream

1 tablespoon mint, chopped

Directions:

In your blender, combine the apples with the cream and mint, pulse well, divide into small cups and serve cold.

Nutrition: calories 70, fat 9, fiber 3, carbs 4.4, protein 3

Rhubarb Pudding

Preparation Time: 10 minutes

Cooking Preparation Time: 20 minutes

Servings: 6

Ingredients:

2 cups rhubarb, sliced

2 tablespoons maple syrup

3 eggs

2 tablespoons coconut oil, melted

1 cup almond milk

½ teaspoon baking powder

Directions:

In a blender, combine the rhubarb with the oil and maple syrup and pulse well.

In a bowl, combine the rhubarb puree with the other ingredients, whisk, divide into 6 ramekins and bake at 350 degrees F for 20 minutes.

Serve the pudding cold.

Nutrition: calories 220, fat 12, fiber 3, carbs 7, protein 8

Pears Cake

Preparation Time: 10 minutes

Cooking Preparation Time: 30 minutes

Servings: 6

Ingredients:

2 pears, cored, peeled and chopped

2 cups coconut flour

1 cup dates, pitted

2 eggs, whisked

1 teaspoon vanilla extract

1 teaspoon baking soda

½ cup coconut oil, melted

½ teaspoon cinnamon powder

Directions:

In a bowl, combine the pears with the flour and the other ingredients, whisk well, pour into a cake pan and bake at 360 degrees F for 30 minutes.

Cool down, slice and serve.

Nutrition: calories 160, fat 7, fiber 4, carbs 8, protein 4.

Dark Chocolate Almond Butter Crunch Balls

Preparation Time: 15 minutes

Cooking Preparation Time: 10 minutes

Servings: 20

Ingredients:

1 cup almond butter, organic and unsweetened

4 tablespoons raw honey

3 tablespoons coconut flour

6 tablespoons rolled oats

½ tablespoon coconut oil

¾ cup dark chocolate chips

Directions:

In a bowl, mix the almond butter and honey until well combined.

Stir in the coconut flour and add oats. Season with salt to taste.

Shape into small balls and place in the fridge to allow to set.

Meanwhile, place the coconut oil in a double boiler and allow to melt. Add in the chocolate chips.

Once melted, dip the balls into the melted chocolate.

Place on a parchment lined tray and allow to set in the fridge for 20 minutes.

Nutrition:

Calories 141, Total Fat 9g, Saturated Fat 3g, Total Carbs 11g, Net Carbs 9g, Protein 4g, Sugar: 7g, Fiber: 2g, Sodium: 27mg, Potassium 321mg

Easy Peach Cobbler

Preparation Time: 15 minutes

Cooking Time:20 minutes

Servings: 6

Ingredients:

5 organic peaches, pitted and chopped

¼ cup coconut palm sugar, divided

½ teaspoon cinnamon

¾ cup chopped pecans

½ cup gluten-free oats

¼ cup ground flaxseeds

¼ brown rice flour

¼ cup extra virgin olive oil

Directions:

Preheat the oven to 3500F.

Grease the bottom of 6 ramekins.

In a bowl, mix the peaches, ½ of the coconut sugar, cinnamon and pecans.

Distribute the peach mixture into the ramekins.

In the same bowl, mix the oats, flaxseed, rice flour, and oil. Add in the remaining coconut sugar. Mix until a crumbly texture is formed.

Top the mixture over the peaches.

Place for 20 minutes.

Nutrition:

Calories 266, Total Fat 11g, Saturated Fat 2g, Total Carbs 28g, Net Carbs 22 g, Protein 10g, Sugar: 12g, Fiber: 6g, Sodium: 127mg, Potassium 440mg

Avocado Chocolate Mousse

Preparation Time: 10 minutes

Cooking Preparation Time: 0 minutes

Servings: 9

Ingredients:

3 ripe avocado, pitted and flesh scooped out

6 ounces plain Greek yogurt

1 bar dark chocolate

1/8 cup unsweetened almond milk

¼ cup ground espresso beans

2 tablespoons raw honey

1 teaspoon vanilla extract

¼ cup cocoa powder

½ teaspoon salt

Directions:

Place all ingredients in a food processor.

Pulse until smooth.

Chill in the fridge before serving.

Nutrition:

Calories 208, Total Fat 15g, Saturated Fat 4g, Total Carbs 17g, Net Carbs 11g, Protein 5g, Sugar: 8g, Fiber: 6g, Sodium: 16mg, Potassium 500mg

Anti-Inflammatory Easy Brownies

Preparation Time: 15 minutes

Cooking Preparation Time: 35 minutes

Servings: 12

Ingredients:

¼ cup ground flaxseed meal

½ cup almond butter

1 ½ cups raw honey

1 teaspoon vanilla extract

¾ cup cocoa powder

1 cup almond flour

1 teaspoon baking powder

¾ cup water

½ teaspoon salt

Directions:

Preheat the oven to 3500F.

In a bowl, mix the flaxseed meal and water. Set aside for 5 minutes.

In a bigger bowl, combine the almond butter, honey, and vanilla extract. Stir to combine.

In another bowl, combine the cocoa powder, almond flour, baking powder, and salt.

Gradually add the wet ingredients to the dry ingredients. Fold until well combined.

Transfer the batter into greased baking pan and spread evenly.

Bake for 35 minutes or until the sides are coming away from the pan.

Allow to cool before slicing.

Nutrition:

Calories 225, Total Fat 8g, Saturated Fat 1g, Total Carbs 41g, Net Carbs 37g, Protein 4g, Sugar: 36g, Fiber: 4g, Sodium: 27mg, Potassium 265mg

Banana Coconut Foster

Preparation Time: 5 minutes

Cooking Preparation Time: 1 hour and 30 minutes

Servings: 6

Ingredients:

10 small cooking bananas, peeled and sliced into quarters

½ cup chopped walnuts

1 cup coconut flakes

1 teaspoon cinnamon

¼ cup honey

½ cup coconut oil, melted

2 teaspoons lemon zest

¼ cup lemon juice

1 teaspoon vanilla extract

Coconut cream for serving

Directions:

Place the bananas in a slow cooker and top with walnuts and coconuts.

In a bowl, combine the cinnamon, honey, coconut oil, lemon zest, lemon juice, and vanilla extract.

Pour the wet mixture over the bananas.

Cook for 1 ½ hour in the slow cooker until the bananas are tender.

Serve with coconut cream on top.

Nutrition:

Calories 463, Total Fat 27g, Saturated Fat 5g, Total Carbs 60g, Net Carbs 53g, Protein 3g, Sugar: 38g, Fiber:7 g, Sodium:43 mg, Potassium 706mg

Antioxidant Chocolate Bites

Preparation Time: 40 minutes

Cooking Preparation Time: 0 minutes

Servings: 6

Ingredients:

½ cup organic unrefined coconut oil

½ cup organic and unsweetened cocoa powder

½ cup organic maple syrup

1 teaspoon vanilla

¼ cup crushed macadamia nuts

¼ cup shredded coconut flakes

¼ cup goji berries

Directions:

In a stove, melt the coconut oil. Set aside.

Put the cocoa powder, maple syrup, vanilla, and melted coconut. Blend well.

Pour into a bowl. Add in the rest of the ingredients.

Mix to combine and form small balls using your hands.

Allow to chill before serving.

Nutrition:

Calories 303, Total Fat 24g, Saturated Fat 5g, Total Carbs 24g, Net Carbs 21g, Protein 2g, Sugar: 18g, Fiber: 3g, Sodium: 15mg, Potassium 270mg

Anti-Inflammatory Apricot Squares

Preparation Time: 60 minutes

Cooking Preparation Time: 0 minutes

Servings: 8

Ingredients:

1 cup dried shredded coconut

1 cup dried apricot, chopped

1 cup raw macadamia nuts, chopped

1 tablespoons coconut oil, melted

1/3 cup turmeric powder

1 teaspoon vanilla extract

Directions:

Combine all ingredients in a food processor until slightly smooth.

Pour mixture into a square pan and press evenly.

Refrigerate for an hour before cutting into squares.

Nutrition:

Calories 201, Total Fat 15g, Saturated Fat 4g, Total Carbs 18g, Net Carbs 14g, Protein 3g, Sugar: 11g, Fiber: 4g, Sodium: 36mg, Potassium 455mg

Anti-Inflammatory Lemon Pudding

Preparation Time: 60 minutes

Cooking Preparation Time: 5minutes

Servings: 6

Ingredients:

2 tablespoons agar flakes

1 cup organic yogurt

½ cup flax oil

¾ cup softened coconut butter

Zest from 3 lemons

1 tablespoon vanilla extract

2 tablespoons coconut oil, melted

½ teaspoon ground cardamom

½ cup raw honey

¼ cup water

1/8 teaspoon salt

Directions:

Heat water in a saucepan until it boils. Remove from the heat and add the agar flakes. Turn on the heat and boil until agar dissolves. Set aside.

In a small bowl, mix everything until well combined.

Pour into glasses.

Place in the fridge to set before serving.

Nutrition:

Calories 521, Total Fat 47g, Saturated Fat 5g, Total Carbs 26g, Net Carbs 25.9g, Protein 2g, Sugar: 25g, Fiber: 0.1g, Sodium: 94mg, Potassium 203mg

Conclusion

I really hope you found this book informative and able to provide you with all of the tools you need to achieve your health goals and discover a different, healthier way to eat.

The scope of this book is to provide you with nutritional information about the anti-inflammatory diet that will grant you so many health benefits and may even save someone's life. By following this diet you will definitely experience a healthier lifestyle that will also prevent chronic illnesses and increase the quality of your life, that is what we are promoting the most with the anti-inflammatory diet.

The next step is to start using the information presented in this book and begin incorporating it into your everyday life. We spoke extensively in this Book about the inflammatory disease and how to prevent or resolve it with a proper diet.

The anti-inflammatory diet will provide you with nutritious and delicious meals. Include it in your own meal prep and create a daily, weekly, or monthly meal schedule so you can stay ahead of the game. Avoiding serious health consequences is an important part of living a long and productive life. A proper diet is instrumental in creating that life for all of us. We know that we were oftentimes blunt when going over information in this book. But we want to make sure people understand the risks of inflammatory disease and the importance of an anti-inflammatory diet.

Now you know everything you need to start the anti-inflammatory diet and reap all of the health benefits that's included. Changing over to this diet doesn't have to be hard.

Just take it one step at a time! Remember that you want to fit the anti-inflammatory diet into your lifestyle and not try to change your lifestyle to fit the diet. Set yourself up with success by planning at least a week in advance, and try new recipes. Even if you don't like them, you at least explored new options and can focus on the recipes you do enjoy while expanding your taste buds.

If you write it down, you are more likely to do it. You are more likely to do something if you get some type of enjoyment out of it.

Enjoy it then!

Try the recipes in this book, get creative with your own recipes, do even more research, and just have fun eating great food.

It may seem like a chore at first. Change is never easy, but oftentimes, it is for the better, especially with matters regarding our health. Trust me, chronic inflammatory disease is no laughing matter.

It is a disease that causes much suffering and can lead to many health problems down the line. Avoid these at all costs by sticking to an anti-inflammatory diet.

The benefits will be tremendous!

Cheers To a healthier lifestyle and good food!

Printed in Great Britain
by Amazon